CAMPING SECRETS

CAMPING SECRETS

A Lexicon of Camping Tips Only the Experts Know

Cliff Jacobson

ICS BOOKS, Inc.
Merrillville, Indiana

CAMPING SECRETS
Copyright © 1987 by Cliff Jacobson

10 9 8 7 6 5 4 3 2

Printed in U.S.A.

Published by:
ICS Books, Inc.
One Tower Plaza
Merrillville, IN 46410

Library of Congress Catalog-in-Publication Data

Jacobson, Cliff.
    Camping secrets / Cliff Jacobson.
        p.   cm.
    Includes index.
    ISBN 0-934802-30-0 : $7.95
    1. Camping 2. Hiking I. Title.
    GV191.7.J33 1987
    796.54--dc19   87-12533
                                                       CIP

Table of Contents

DEDICATION

To my friend, Chic Sheridan — able woodsman and the best
scoutmaster I ever knew.

What! Another Camping Book?

Camping out has changed considerably from the good old days of pine bough beds, bonfires and fresh-cut trail shelters. No longer is it ethical to shape the land to suit our whims. There are just too few wild places and too many of us!

As a result, a whole new style of camping has evolved — one geared to the high-tech lightweight equipment of today. Forty pound canvas tents have been thoughtfully replaced by equally spacious nylon models of one-fourth the weight. Camp stoves have taken over where fires once ruled, and a deluge of new fabrics — polypropylene, polyester pile, orlon acrylics and Gore-Tex, have challenged traditional fibers. Packsacks, hiking boots, raingear — everything has become lighter, more compact and reliable. Surprisingly good outdoor gear can now be purchased at big city discount stores — testimony to the growing interest in camping out.

Amidst the generally welcome improvements in gear, the one thing that has not changed at all is "knowledge" of the sport. The wise old scoutmaster who could sniff a coming storm and rig a tight camp in a driving rain, has all but been replaced by the well-meaning leader who atones the night in his pick-up camper...or more likely, doesn't camp at all. Everyone, it seems, has plenty of gear to cope with the elements, but precious few know how to use it. If misery loves company, you'll find plenty of it in the backcountry. Just watch the campers roll home (or to the nearest motel) at the first sight of rain. The notion that bad weather spells bad times afield is so firmly entrenched in the minds of modern man that it is probably pointless for me to argue "the truth" in the pages of this book. Nonetheless, I shall try.

This book is not intended to take the place of a "sport-specific" text on backpacking, canoeing, family camping or the like. Rather, it details hundreds of ideas and procedures which are never found in traditional camping texts — ideas which will make your next campout safer and more enjoyable. Everything has been alphabetized and indexed for your convenience, and space-consuming anecdotes have been eliminated to make room for the obscure but important things you really need to know.

Some of you may recognize procedures from my books *Canoeing Wild Rivers,* and *The New Wilderness Canoeing & Camping.* These are repeated here for the benefit of those who don't canoe. After all, the rules of backcountry comfort are the same whether you travel by foot, ski, canoe or truck camper. Foul weather can make you just as miserable in a state park camp ground as on a remote canoe trail.

Here's wishing you warm winds, fair weather and bug-free days, and enough good camping skills to cope with the worst of times on the best of terms.

Credits

I wish to express thanks to the following people for their support and encouragement:

My publisher, Dr. Bill Forgey and editor Tom Todd, who from the beginning believed in the value of this book. *Canoe* Magazine for use of my article "Rope Tricks," which appeared in October, 1984. To Lisa Billingham, Bob Brown, Fred Cole, Jim and Verna Robinson, and my wife Sharon and daughters Clarissa and Peggy, for their helpful suggestions. And especially to Dr. Tom Schwinghamer, CEO of River Valley Clinic, Hastings, Minnesota, for his practical tips on woods medicine.

Anchor

Here's a slick way to make a light, portable anchor for fishing in a canoe. All you need is a basketball net and carabiner (an aluminum link used by mountaineers — available at most camp shops). Tie off the net bottom with cord. Fill the net with rocks then gather the net perimeter and clip it together with the carabiner. Attach a rope to the carabiner and you're set for action.

Animals

Bears and other beasts

Background: Each year, thousands of campers lose food and equipment to persistent bears, raccoons, ground squirrels and other animals. The common advice is to protect foodstuffs by one of these methods:

1. Store food inside your car.
2. Suspend food cache-like from a tree limb at least 20 feet above the ground. Here are the realities and hazards of each method:

Store food inside your car

This is acceptable even in grizzly country providing you take care to seal *all* car windows tightly. Bears (especially grizzlies)

1

will insert their claws through the tiniest openings in windows and doors and rip out the glass or metal to get at food. Today's hardtop cars make it relatively easy for a determined bruin to steal food. For this reason, a car trunk is safer than an auto interior.

Expert campers usually *do not* store their food in trees to protect it from bears. Instead, they seal the food tightly in plastic to eliminate odors then remove the food from the immediate camp area. Setting the food pack *outside* the campsite perimeter is usually enough to foil hungry bruins and other animals. The rationale for this procedure is simple: Bears are creatures of habit — they quickly learn that camps, packs and tin cans contain food. In each campsite there is usually only one or two trees with limbs high enough to confidently suspend food packs. But bears aren't stupid; they know the location of these trees by heart and make daily rounds to secure whatever is suspended from them. When they find something (anything!) hanging from "their" tree, they'll get it down, one way or another. All black bears (even fat old sows) can climb to some degree. And cubs shinny like monkeys. If momma can't get your food pack, the kids probably will! Only polar bears and grizzlies don't climb.

Recommendation: Double bag (in plastic) all foodstuffs, especially meats. Set food packs on *low ground* (to minimize the travel of odors) well away from the confines of the campsite. Separate food packs by 50 feet or more, as an added precaution. *Do not*, as commonly advised, put food packs in trees!

Raccoons and ground squirrels: A plastic or metal ice chest will protect foodstuffs from ravaging raccoons and ground squirrels, but there is no acceptable portable container that will reliably discourage bears. Ground squirrels and raccoons have very sharp teeth and will bore right through a fabric packsack. Best recommendation is to store food in vehicle trunks or on the ground, outside campsite areas. Caching food from high trees is a good idea only in infrequented wilderness. Even then, it's a waste of time unless you'll be separated from your food supply for long periods of time.

Bear encounters: Here's the recommended procedure in the event you meet face to face with ...

A black bear

Blackies are timid and will ordinarily run away at the first smell of you. Bears don't see very well; what most people interpret as a "charge" is usually nothing more than simple curiosity. Screaming, blowing whistles and other noise-making will usually send a wild bear running, but an experienced camp bear will remain totally oblivious to the racket. Best procedure is to hold your ground, spread your arms wide (so you look bigger), talk authoritatively and back off slowly. *Do not* run!

The danger signs are "woofing" and "clacking." If the bear goes "woof, woof, woof" and you hear loud hicupping sounds with the clacking of teeth, the situation is deteriorating. The bear's mad and unpredictable. If there's a tree handy, climb it now. If you can beat a path to safer ground, go for it. But remember, your safe haven better be close because you can't outrun the bear by far! Failing this, hold the bluff as long as you dare, then assume a fetal position, hands clasped tightly behind your neck, and *play dead.*

Grizzlies

Grizzlies have been clocked at 45 miles per hour on flat terrain. No way can you outrun one. Again, these are shy animals; they should instantly run away from you. Grizzlies are king of the hill in their domain; it's doubtful you can bluff them. I was once charged by three grizzlies on the open tundra of Canada and can personally attest to the worth of the following system:

1.   Talk in a moderate, unthreatening tone to the bear. Let him/her know you're there. Get the bear's attention without intimidating him.

2.   If the bear runs towards you, interpret this as curiosity, not as a "charge." Remember, bears don't see very well, and they can't smell you if you're downwind.

3.   When the bear is within 50 feet, drop to the ground, assume a tight fetal position, play absolutely dead ... and pray! My bears came within a dozen feet, checked me out, then high-tailed it over the next hill. "Your" bear will likely do the same.

Polar bears

Good luck! These are fast on the flats and can swim four or five miles per hour for hours on end in ice water. They will, on rare occasions, eat human flesh. They have been known to stalk humans! Nonetheless, most polar bears will do their best to steer clear of you. It's best you do likewise. You cannot intimidate or outrun these animals. And in their habitat there is usually no place to hide. You are at their mercy.

A final note: Desk-bound environmentalists would have you believe that all wild animals are harmless, while Rambo- survivalists will suggest the opposite. Facts suggest you are more at risk when crossing a four lane highway than in a face to face encounter with a bear. Nonetheless. some critters, like some people, are plainly crazy and quite unpredictable. So beware of the approximate one percent of bears who don't share your live and let live approach. Don't over-react to bear encounters; just follow the recommended guidelines. And be aware that you are much safer in seldom traveled wilderness than in heavily used national parks where bears are used to the sight of people.

Axe

Background: The trend today is against use of axes in the backcountry. The argument is that they are more often used to deface green trees and injure people than to produce firewood. In truth, it is not the tool that is dangerous, it is the person who wields it. Outdoor experts value a good sharp axe. They know it is much simpler to produce fire after a week long rain if a splitting tool of some sort is available.

What size axe? Old time camping books suggest use of the full length to three-quarter size axe under the guise these are safer than the short hand axe (hatchet). Hogwash! A *properly used* hand-axe is the safest of all edged tools; it is lighter and more compact than a large axe, and when used in conjunction with a folding saw, it will produce all the camp wood you need with surprisingly little effort.

Here are the rules for safe, efficient use of the handaxe:

1.   Saw (see section on "saws") wood to be split into 12 inch lengths.

2.   Use the handaxe as a *splitting wedge. Do not* chop with it! The folding saw performs *all* cutting functions.

3.   Set the axe head lightly into the end grain of the wood (Figure A-1). One person holds the tool while a friend pounds it through with a chunk of log. All-steel handaxes are better for this than those with wooden handles as they are less apt to break. When

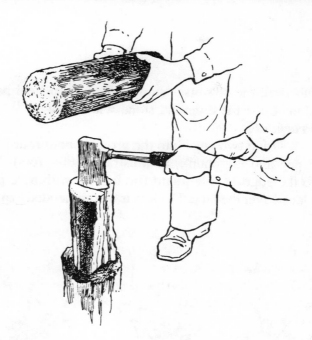

Figure A-1.

splitting very thick (over 6 inches) logs, take multiple splittings off the edges.

Safety concerns: Hold the axe solidly with *both* hands. Allow the log hammer to do all the work.

4. *To produce kindling:* Kindling splits easiest from the end grain, a process that's made easier and safer if you use a stick of wood to hold the upright in place (Figure A-2).

Sharpening: You'll need a flat mill file and a soft Arkansas or diamond stone. Use special cutting oil, WD-40, or kerosine to

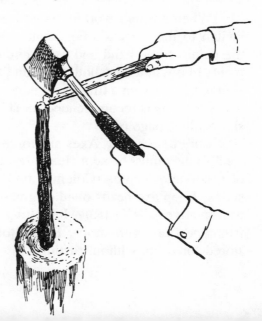

Figure A-2.

lubricate the Arkansas stone and to keep steel particles in suspension. Lube the diamond stone with water.

Procedure

Drive two pegs into the ground about four inches apart, or use a peg and log chunk, as illustrated (Fig. A-3). File *perpendicular* to the edge. A file guard (tin can lid with hole punched in center) placed over the rat tail handle is recommended to prevent cut fingers.

Figure A-3.

When a rough working edge has been obtained with the file, switch to the stone(s). For greatest safety, hold the axe blade in the palm of one hand and use a *circular* motion of the stone. Use plenty of oil, and wipe both stone and axe edge frequently to remove filings. If you want a fine, razor edge, stone the blade perpendicular to the edge as is recommended for sharpening the knife (see Knife, sharpening, page 62).

Care of the axe: Axes are forged from relatively soft carbon steel so they must be kept clean, dry, and rust-free. A small amount of gasoline or naptha (Coleman fuel) will remove pitch and wood stains. Keep axe heads oiled or greased when not in use. Best rust preventative is RIG (Rust Inhibiting Grease) Universal, available from sport and gun shops. Edged tools coated with RIG may be stored for years without rusting.

Blueing the head: Most axes have painted heads to minimize rust. For ease of maintenance and beauty, grind off the paint, buff the head, and apply cold gun blue to the bright metal. The axe head will develop a mildly rust-resistant blue-black sheen, which is instantly restored by dabbing on more blue gun (available at most hardware/sports shops).

Sheathing the axe: Sheaths which come with edged tools are usually too thin and flimsy for practical field service. Make your own as follows:

1.   Obtain two pieces of one-eighth inch thick sole leather from a leather company or your shoemaker.

2.   Soak the leather in warm water until it is soft, then cut two matching pieces as shown in Figure A-4.

3.   Contact cement (I suggest *Weldwood* Contact Cement) a one-quarter inch wide strip of leather all around the edge. Then rivet on a buckle or Velcro security strap and contact cement the sheath halves together. Rivet the edges of the sheath for greatest security, or have your shoe repair man sew it for you. Two-piece hammer driven rivets can be purchased from every leather supply store. Handaxes are never carried on the belt so no belt loop is necessary.

Figure A-4. The heavy sole leather sheaths shown here require less than one hour of time to make. Leather and rivets can be purchased by mail from several leather companies. *Photo by Mark Lindeck*

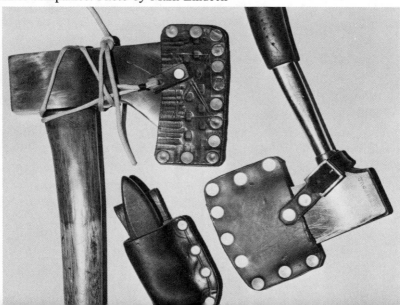

Making a permanently bonded head: Camping books traditionally suggest that you occasionally soak the heads of wood-handled axes in water or oil to expand the handle eye so the head won't come loose. The "water treatment" is dreadfully temporary; oil works only marginally better. Here's a permanent solution:

1.   Use a very blunt screwdriver or edge of a flat file as a wedge to drive the factory installed wooden wedge tightly into the handle eye. You should be able to sink the factory wedge a full one-quarter to one-third inch below the level of the steel axe head.

2.   Drive a small steel wedge solidly into the heart of the sunken wooden wedge. The steel wedge will not go in all the way but its head must be below the level of the steel axe head.

3.   Fill the void (trench) with slow cure or five-minute epoxy. You now have a permanently bonded head which will never come loose.

Baking

Background: Reflector ovens and double-pan Dutch ovens are traditional for backcountry baking. However, both require a good hot fire or glowing coals. Modern campers rely almost exclusively on stoves for all their cooking so the oven should reflect this change in style. Here are some untraditional baking ideas:

The Jello-mold oven: You'll need a wide ring aluminum Jello mold and a cover of some sort (Fig. B-1).

1. Grease the mold and put your batter into the outside ring. Decrease the suggested amount of water by up to one-fourth for faster baking.

2. "Large-burner" stoves like the Coleman Peak 1 and double-burner models, may burn the edges of the bakestuff. An electric the Jello mold over the burner head, top it with a high cover (necessary to allow sufficient room for the bake-good to rise) and relax. Cooking times are nearly identical to those suggested in the baking directions.

3. Cool the mold by setting it in a shallow pan of water for a few moments, then pop out your entree.

Figure B-1. The Jello mold.

Tips

1. Wind reduces the efficiency of the Jello mold, so use a good windshield around your stove.

2. "Large-burner" stoves like the Coleman Peak 1 and double- burner models, may burn the edges of the bakestuff. An electric stove burner shield, available for a few dollars at most supermarkets, will eliminate this problem. Simply place the shield under the Jello mold. The air space between the shield and mold bottom will prevent burning. The large size burner shield will fit large ring Jello molds perfectly.

Other uses of the jello mold

Your Jello mold may also be used as a steamer to rehydrate dried fruits and vegetables. Here's how: 1.   Place dried fruit or beans in the Jello mold ring with about two tablespoons of water.

2.   Fill a stainless-steel cup with water and set it on the chimney of the mold.

3.   Cover the mold and cup and turn the stove to medium-high. Boiling water from the Sierra cup will vaporize and steam your fruit or vegetables to tenderness in a fraction the time of simple soaking. It's the steam that does the trick!

You can also fire the Jello mold with a small (2-5/8 ounce) can of Sterno or an aluminum 35 mm film can filled with rubbing alcohol. Don't use the large size cans of Sterno; they put out too much heat. To ensure ample draft, use a pair of half-inch diameter sticks to prop the ring above the Sterno. You must ventilate the high cover with a match stick or the Sterno (or alcohol) will go out.

You may also use the Jello mold as a "pot support" on your stove. To heat a single cup of water on your trail stove, set a water-filled Sierra cup into the Jello mold chimney. A cover will speed heating and save stove fuel.

*Triple-pan method of baking on your stove:*Use this method if you don't have a Jello mold. You'll need two nesting skillets, a high cover and a half dozen small nails or stones.

1.   Evenly scatter the nails or stones onto the surface of the large (bottom) frying pan.

2.   Place your bakestuff into the small frying pan and set it on top of the nails (the two pans must be separated by nails or stones to prevent burning).

3.   Cover the unit and place it on your stove. Use the lowest possible blue-flame setting.

Warning: Don't use this method with a thin aluminum skillet on the bottom; you'll burn a hole right through it!

Binoculars

Binoculars are worth bringing along on wilderness canoe trips. They enable you to quickly locate portage trails and campsites on complex lakes and they are a wonderful tool for checking rapids. A monocular is not good enough; you need "two eye" depth perception for interpreting river dangers.

Boots

Background: Camping footwear is in revolution. Where, a decade ago, heavy four pound/pair boots with lugged soles were the norm, today's hiker chooses the lightest most flexible footwear he/she can find. The trend began when we quit thumbing our noses at primitive peoples, Indians and Eskimos who routinely traveled the most difficult terrain while wearing moccasins, sandals, and no

shoes at all. The coup de grace was quietly administered when
American and British mountaineers were out-footed by sandal-wear-
ing sherpas who casually carried loads far in excess of those toted
by well-heeled climbers. Specialized lightweight running shoes set
the trend; featherweight hiking boots logically followed suit.

Which boots for you? There are boots of all leather, leather
and nylon, pure (synthetic) rubber, or leather-rubber combinations,
like the L.L. Bean Maine hunting shoe. There's also a diversity of
unique winter wear. Here are the differences:

Combination leather/nylon boots are light, supple, comfortable, and most popular. They require almost no break-in. The best
models are suitable for the most strenuous off-trail applications,
with the exception of rock-climbing or boulder-scree hiking. Unfortunately, most of these "combo" boots cannot be re-soled when
they wear out — a factor to consider if you'll subject them to heavy
use.

Supple, all leather boots which can be re-soled (check 'em
out, most can't!) are the sturdiest, most reliable, and probably the
best buy. All leather boots will outlast leather/fabric combos by
decades.

Gore-Tex liners: Some of the best boots (especially leather/fab-
ric ones) come with liners of breathable, waterproof Gore-Tex.
Though Gore-Tex liners perform admirably over the short haul,
they may not be reliable in the long run. If the Gore-Tex liner in
a fabric foot fails, you're doomed to wet feet — an instant displea-
sure the moment you walk through dew-moistened grass. Traditional
all-leather boots can be made acceptably water-resistant by judicious
application of wax or grease, but fabric ones cannot.

Despite convincing advertising, Gore-Tex has not proven reliable enough for day-in day-out use in wet country. And neither has
any brand of all-leather boots. If you want truly waterproof footwear, follow the lead of lobster fishermen and Alaskan guides, and
select *all-rubber* boots. For occasionally wet weather — stepping
in and out of water — the vote goes to the leather/rubber "Maine
Hunting Shoe" offered by L.L. Bean (L.L. Bean, Inc. Freeport,
Maine 04033), which incidentally comes in sizes to fit women and
children.

To break in new boots:
1. By the traditional method: Wear boots an hour or two

each day until they fit properly. This painful procedure takes about a week.

2. The preferred method: Fill each new boot level full of luke-warm tap water. Allow the water to soak in for about 15 seconds then pour it out. Now put on the boots (with the correct socks, of course) and walk them dry — takes about three hours and results in about 50 percent break-in. Wear the boots around the house for about an hour each day for a week following the "water treatment" and they'll be sufficiently broken in for hiking.

Care of boots: Sponge dirt and grime off leather boots with saddle soap and water. Work up a good lather then remove the suds with a damp sponge. It's not necessary to get all the soap out. Gentle sponging with plain soap and water is the best way to clean the fabric panels on leather/fabric boots.

Allow boots to dry thoroughly away from heat then apply an oil-based preservative like "Mink Oil" (with or without silicone) to oil-tanned leather. Apply a wax-based compound like "Snow Seal" to chrome-tanned leather. It's important to realize that waxes do a much better job of waterproofing than oils and greases designed for use on oil-tanned leather. Fortunately, waxes are compatible with oils and greases if used sparingly. I've found that you can improve the weather resistance of oil-tanned boots considerably by topping the oil base (which should be well absorbed into the leather pores) with "Snow Seal" or "Bee Seal."

To apply boot grease or wax: Melt the preservative (leave the tin in hot sunlight for a few minutes) and apply it to lightly warmed leather with your bare hands. Rub in thoroughly and allow boots to "sun-bathe" until excess preservative is absorbed. Repeat application of the product until no excess remains on the leather. A dry rag may be used to remove excess grease which remains after the second application.

To dry wet boots: Never put boots too near a fire (if you can't hold your hand near the flame for 30 seconds, it's too hot for your boots!) or in an oven to dry them. You can speed drying of wet boots by stuffing them with fire-warmed pebbles placed inside socks.

Always carry some "boot wax" in a 35mm film can on all your outings. Apply it frequently in wet weather.

Removing mold from boots and leather gear: Boots and leather goods stored in damp areas (basements) are sure to mold. Best way to remove mold is with a 25 percent solution of vinegar, household ammonia, or oxygen bleach which will go deep into the pores of the leather and kill fungal hyphae. Thoroughly rinse "mold-treated" leather with clear water and allow it to dry before you apply preservatives. Sunlight kills fungous too, so give your leather goods a frequent airing outdoors.

To improve the warmth of boots: Install warm insoles! Toughest and warmest are those which are cut from EVA (ethyl- vinyl-acetate) foam sleeping pads (available at most camp shops). EVA has exceptional strength, abrasion resistance and insulative properties. It's a very exceptional foam! Even pure rubber boots, which are notoriously cold in sub-freezing weather, will become downright toasty when lined with EVA.

Oversocks: If your boots are too small to accept warm insoles, try wearing thick wool socks over them. Of course, the sock bottoms will quickly wear through, but what's left will add considerable warmth. Specialized oversocks are commonly worn over ski boots by cross-country skiers and these can be purchased at most ski shops.

The warmest boots are military surplus all rubber "Mickey Mouse" boots. Mouse boots are cold-proof but very uncomfortable to wear. Pure white "bunny" boots — another surplus item — which are made from wool felt, are wonderfully warm and are great for walking. Wear rubbers or galoshes over them in wet snow.

Canadian "Sorels" or fabric top snowmobile boots are the preferred choice for one day use but become damp after a good workout. The felt liners in these boots *must* be changed daily or frostbite may result.

In summary:

1.   For relatively dry three season use, traditional lightweight all leather boots are best. Combination leather/fabric boots tend to be less waterproof, but lighter, more comfortable and cooler.

2.   For mixed (wet/dry) conditions, leather top/rubber bottom shoe-pacs like traditional L.L. Bean Maine Hunting Shoes work best. "Bean Boots" are the most popular boots in the world. Millions of pairs have been sold ... and re-soled. These are by far the best boots for typical fall hiking and hunting in the wetland states.

3.   Mickey Mouse boots are best for standing around. Sorels or fabric-topped snowmobile boots work well if liners are changed daily.

4.   White bunny boots or felt-lined canvas muklucks (a difficult surplus item to find these days) are the best cold weather combination for dry snow and are the preferred choice of competitive snowshoers.

Bottles

Polyethylene bottles and plastic food tubes

Background: Various sizes and shapes of polyethylene bottles are commonly used by campers to store liquid and semi-liquid foods like jam, peanut butter, pancake syrup and cooking oil. Most of the plastic containers on supermarket shelves are too flimsy for strenuous camping trips; you need thick-walled tough containers for serious backwoods use.

By far, the most reliable containers for foodstuffs are those made by the *Nalgene Company*. Nalgene bottles were originally designed for packaging chemicals, so you know they're bomb-proof. Nalgene containers are positively leakproof and deservedly expensive. All the best camping stores carry them.

Most reliable supermarket bottle I've found is the "Golden Griddle" pancake syrup container which features a "pop-lock" (the top pops up to open) top. Pop-tops of any type are unreliable. Either replace them with metal screw caps (available at wine supply stores) or melt the tops shut in the flame of a gas stove.

Plastic food containers will retain odors after use. A thorough washing won't help much. What will, is a mixture of baking soda and water. Allow the soda/water solution to remain in the bottles for a full two weeks and odors will all but disappear.

Plastic food tubes, which are available at most camping stores, resemble large toothpaste tubes. They are commonly used to hold jam, peanut butter and other "semi-liquids." The tubes are filled from the open back end and are sealed with a marginally effective plastic clip. To use a food tube, unscrew the cap and squeeze the container (like a toothpaste tube). The idea sounds great but the product is unreliable, especially when the tubes are filled more than

two-thirds full. Expert campers don't trust food tubes. I suggest
you don't either!

Bugs

Biting insects: black flies, mosquitoes, noseeums

Colors: Dark colors, especially navy blue and black, attract
insects. Powder blue, yellow, mist-green, white and other light
colors have a neutral or mild repelling effect. Mosquitoes come out
right after a rain, so it's best to avoid dark blue rain suits. Air-force
blue wool pants and shirts are an abomination in the woods and
are nearly impossible to wear on buggy days. Contrary to popular
belief, *red* does not repel black flies. Red is a fairly neutral color
which neither repels nor attracts insects.

Repellents: Best chemical repellent to date is N. N-Diethyl-
metatoluamide, commonly known as DEET. The higher the percen-
tage of DEET, the more effective (and expensive) the repellent.
Products which contain more than 80 percent DEET are highly
effective but may burn sensitive skin, a factor to consider if you're
camping with children.

Best buy in repellents is Vietnam *Jungle Juice*, which is now
commercially marketed under the REI (Recreational Equipment,
Inc. P.O. Box C-88125, Seattle, WA 98188) label. Jungle Juice
is 71.25 percent DEET which is a good compromise between effectiveness and "wearability."

Keep repellents away from plastics: glasses, Swiss army knife
handles and polypropylene underwear will dissolve instantly on
contact. Once a bottle of Jungle Juice leaked through a friend's
trouser pocket. The repellent dissolved a huge swatch of his polypropylene underwear in a most embarrassing place!

Headnets are essential for early season trips in northern Canada.
Best are the old French army style which feature two wide hoops
to keep netting away from your face. Cost is about three dollars at
surplus stores.

Bug-net jackets: The "Shoe-Bug" jacket consists of a net fabric
which is heavily impregnated with DEET. The jacket discourages
insects but some wearers experience allergic reactions to the high
localized concentration of DEET. Some years ago, Johnson Wax
offered a similar Citronella impregnated jacket which was less

allergenic. Johnson Bug jackets are no longer sold in the U.S., but may still be available in Canada.

Noseeums: These tiny biting gnats are small enough to fly through standard mesh bug netting. They bite with a fiery nip. Noseeum tent netting will stop these critters cold; however, noseeum net is so tightly woven that ventilation may be a problem in muggy weather.

Headnets are best constructed of dark-colored standard mesh mosquito net, both for good visibility and ventilation. It's difficult to see through the milk-colored noseeum net supplied with many tents.

Black flies: DEET repellents work marginally well, but head-nets, gloves and tough woven pants and shirts work better. Black flies prefer the constricted areas around wrists, ankles, behind the ear, etc. In black fly areas wear long underwear next to the skin and tuck trousers into boots or "blouse" them over the top with military blousing bands or Velcro tabs. Velcro tabs on shirt cuffs will seal your armor completely.

-   If you lightly saturate a cotton bandanna with insect repellent and tie it around your neck, flying insects will keep reasonably clear of your head.

-   BEN GAY is a surprisingly good insect repellent.

-   Liquid or cream repellents are much more potent (a better buy) than sprays.

-   Household ammonia and water will cut the sting of mosquito bites. For bee, wasp and hornet stings, apply a wet salt pack and allow it to dry. The salt will draw the pain away quickly.

Camera

Waterproof protection: The most waterproof camera container is the *amphibious assault gas mask bag* (a military surplus item). These bags, which are similar to commercial Phoenix brand plastic camera bags, are constructed of heavy rubber covered with 10 ounce canvas duck. Three solid brass fasteners secure the roll-down pouch top. Gas mask bags are absolutely watertight under the most rigorous conditions. Cost is around six dollars at this writing.

Thirty and fifty caliber steel ammunition boxes are commonly used by boaters to protect cameras from water. Check the rubber seals on these boxes; they frequently *are not* watertight! Gas mask bags are cheaper and more reliable containers.

If you're shooting a number of rolls of film and want to keep the order straight, try this: Write the number of each roll (1, 2, 3 etc.) on a slip of paper when you load the film into the camera. Photograph the number on the paper. This will identify the order in which each roll was shot.

Canteen

Only cheechakos and bona-fide cowboys use traditional canteens these days. Expert campers rely on poly bottles to carry thirst quenchers. Plastic bottles are cheaper, lighter and easier-to-pack than metal canteens.

Plastic baby bottles make good canteens, and they fit nicely into the side pockets of small hiking packs.

Fill your canteen four-fifths full of water and freeze it to assure a supply of cold water during the next day's hike.

A glass vacuum bottle, sans cup, makes a surprisingly good canteen. Modern vacuum bottles are quite strong and lightweight; they assure a cold (or hot) drink throughout the day.

The traditional bota, or wine bladder remains popular with skiers. It also makes a fine easy-to-carry canteen for summer hiking.

Here's a good way to warm up your sleeping bag on a cold night: Pour boiling water into your canteen, roll the canteen in a towel or shirt, and take this "hot water bottle" to bed.

Do not put carbonated beverages or alcohol into an aluminum canteen. These products will react with the aluminum!

The tough mylar bag (bladder) which lines Italian Swiss Colony (and some other brands) wine boxes, makes a great "giant" canteen. Sew tough nylon webbing around the bladder (there's plenty of seam allowance) so you can hang the unit from a tree and dispense liquid through the efficient rubber faucet-like spout. Note: the rubber

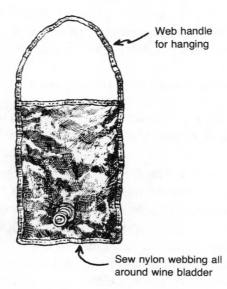

Web handle
for hanging

Sew nylon webbing all
around wine bladder

Figure C-1. The wine bladder canteen.

spouts are easy to remove if you grasp the lip with a thumb nail and pull. No amount of twisting and forcing will break it loose.

Here's how to make a collapsible nylon water bucket:

1.   Cut a three foot diameter circle of waterproof nylon (taffeta or rip-stop).

2.   Gather the circular edge of the material to form a bag, and sew the pleated mouth, leaving an approximate three inch opening.

3.   Sew seam binding all around the mouth of the bag. Sew a handle of nylon webbing across the mouth.

This water bag is very compact. It must be hung from a branch as it is not free-standing.

Car Top Carriers (Canoe Racks)

-   To prevent car top carriers from grooving the gunnels of canoes and boats, wrap them with sections of wet carpeting and coil nylon line tightly around the carpet to hold it in place. When the carpet dries, you'll have a thick, protective non-skid surface.

-   Here's a slick way to pad the tubes of car top carriers which utilize one inch diameter steel conduit stock: Lubricate one inch diameter heater hose with *brake fluid*, then squeeze the heater hose over the steel conduit. The brake fluid will be forced out and the hose will take a permanent custom set, as if it were glued in place. Heater hose does not deteriorate in rain or sun.

Canoe and Boat Rigging Tips*

*See my books, *CANOEING WILD RIVERS* and the *NEW WILDERNESS CANOEING & CAMPING*, for a wealth of detailed canoeing and canoe rigging tips.

-   *Compass*: For ease in navigating complex lakes, secure a wrist compass around the aft canoe thwart. This will enable you to simultaneously paddle and follow a plotted course.

-   *Custom improvements*: Thread loops of fabric shock-cord through holes drilled in the canoe's thwarts and deck plates. End lines (painters) stored under the shock-cord loops will stay put in a capsize and on portages. Oddities may be secured under the thwart cords.

-   Fiberglass and Royalex canoes should have lining holes or rings installed at cutwater, not high on the deck as is the common practice. See Figure C-2.

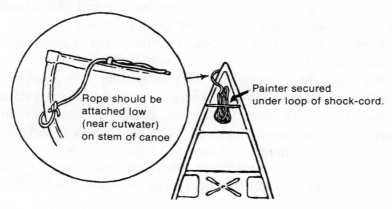

Figure C-2. End lines, shock cords, and lining holes.

-   A two quart plastic water pitcher tied to a canoe thwart makes a handy bailer and is also useful for mixing powdered drinks in camp.

-   Install "pockets" in your canoe or fishing boat. You can purchase commercial models from California Rivers, Inc. P.O. Box 468, Geyserville, CA 95441, or Cooke Custom Sewing, 1544 Osborne Rd NE, Fridley, MN 55432. Or, you can make your own by sewing up an envelope of nylon with elastic or Velcro at the mouth. Boat pockets provide convenient places to store maps, bug dope, sunscreen and other small items.

-   Varnish caned canoe seats before you use them the first time. The varnish will eliminate sag and considerably prolong the life of the cane.

-   Drill holes in canoe and boat seats so they won't pool water when it rains.

-   Glue (contact cement) EVA (ethyl-vinyl-acetate) foam to the surface of canoe and boat seats to increase comfort and warmth. The foam will also add flotation to the craft.

-   The only emergency repair kit you really need for a canoe or boat is a roll of 2-inch wide silver duct tape. Duct tape sticks to anything. Use it for emergency repairs to all your camping gear.

- Paint decks on aluminum canoes flat black to reduce glare.
- For kneeling comfort when paddling, glue foam knee pads into your canoe. Best foam for this purpose is EVA (ethyl-vinyl-acetate), available at camping stores. Weldwood contact cement is the most reliable adhesive and will work on any surface.

Tying canoes on cars: Best hitch for this is the "power cinch." See knots, page 67.

Yoke: A yoke is essential if you plan to carry your canoe alone for even short distances. A curved hardwood yoke, with overstuffed foam-filled shoulder pads, is the most comfortable combination. Commercial yokes cost upwards of 40 dollars and are seldom very good. You can make a much better yoke than you can buy.

Make your yoke from white ash (preferred) (Fig. C-3) and finish to the dimensions illustrated. The completed yoke should

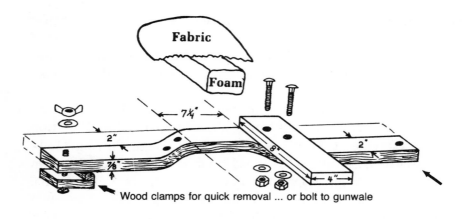

Figure C-3. A homemade yoke with drainage holes will take the sting out of a long carry.

have some flex which will take the sting out of a rigorous carry. Use open cell polyurethane foam (pillow padding) for the shoulder pads. Naugahyde or other heavy plastic upholstery material is the best covering fabric. Attach the yoke to the balance point of the canoe (some prefer a slightly tail heavy arrangement) with bolts or wood clamps. The clamp and wingnut set-up is best if you plan to carry a third person in the canoe. You can easily remove the yoke to provide more room for your passenger.

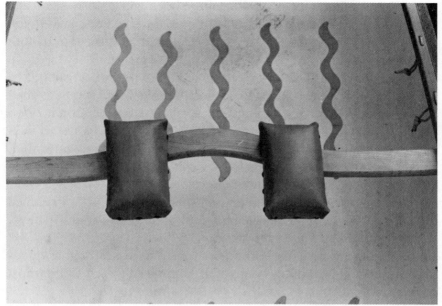

Figure C-4. A curved hardwood yoke with overstuffed foam-filled shoulder pads is the most comfortable device for carrying a canoe.

Children

Tips for camping with ...

Rain Gear: Best rain gear for young children is an inexpensive plastic poncho, coated nylon windbreaker, and a souwester style hat. Trim the poncho to fit with a scissors. Waterproof the stitching of the coated jacket with seam sealant (every camp shop has it). Be sure to glue the seams on the souwester hat too.

Rationale: The youngster wears the coated wind-shell under the poncho — it keeps arms dry and provides a secondary "drip" layer in prolonged rain. The souwester hat is worn *over* the poncho hood and is tied beneath the chin. Together, these garments provide serviceable and very inexpensive protection from rain.

Emergency rain gear for kids (or adults) may be fashioned from a large leaf and lawn size garbage bag. Cut head and arm holes, provide a souwester hat, and you'll stay reasonably dry.

Wet weather foot gear: Running shoes and galoshes, or any rubber boots sized large enough to fit over the sneakers, are all you need. When rains quit, the boots are removed and freedom of foot is instantly restored.

Camp clothing: Cotton clothing (except underwear) should be avoided except in the predictable heat of mid-July. Woolens may be too scratchy for some youngsters, so the logical solution is *orlon acrylics*. Acrylic sweaters, gloves and hats dry quickly after a wetting and retain their insulative properties when damp or soiled. Acrylic garments are also quite inexpensive; they are ideal for spring canoe and boat trips, for adults as well as kids.

Hats: Kids need three hats on a camping trip — a brimmed cap for sun, a warm stocking cap (wool or acrylic) for chilly days, and the traditional souwester for rain.

Sleeping gear: Kids *do not* need air mattresses or foam pads for comfort. Their young bones will happily conform to the most uneven ground!

You must provide a foam pad (not an air mattress — these *conduct* cold!) if down sleeping bags are used. Body weight compresses the underside of a down bag to near zero thickness and chilling will result unless insulation is provided. The typical polyester (Polarguard, Quallofil or Hollofil) sleeping bag provides sufficient insulation below so that, except in very cold weather, mattresses may be omitted.

Sleeping bags are unnecessary for typical summer camping. One or two light wool or fluffy acrylic blankets, folded as illustrated (Figure C-5), will provide plenty of warmth in temperatures to 45 degrees.

Increasing warmth of a sleeping bag: The warmth of a sleeping bag is partly related to the amount of space the body has to heat. by reducing dead air space, you'll increase warmth. Figure C-6 shows an easy way to reduce the dimensions, and add warmth, to the typical station-wagon sized sleeping bag. A flannel "draft collar" sewn to the top of a sleeping bag will increase warmth considerably.

Insects (see BUGS, page 16) A headnet is a wise investment if you'll be camping in buggy country. Choose mild, cream-base repellents rather than more powerful chemicals which may "burn" sensitive young skin.

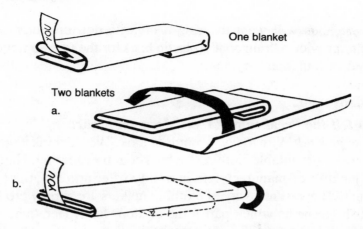

One blanket

Two blankets
a.

b.

Figure C-5. For summer use, blankets will work as well as a sleeping bag. Here's how to fold them for maximum warmth.

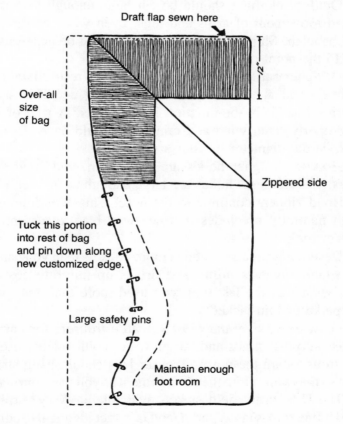

Draft flap sewn here

Over-all
size
of bag

12"

Zippered side

Tuck this portion
into rest of bag
and pin down along
new customized edge.

Large safety pins

Maintain enough
foot room

Figure C-6. Customizing a sleeping bag for children.

Toys: Kids will want to bring a favorite doll or teddy bear. Be sure to provide a "rain coat" (plastic bag) for the toy, so it won't be ruined in foul weather.

Clothing

How to tell the "real thing" from designer wear!

Background: With today's "outdoor look," you'd think it would be easy to locate suitable clothing for backcountry camping. Hardly! Only a handful of manufacturers currently offer attire that is truly functional. The vast majority of clothing makers are simply producing stylish garments which parrot the outdoor look. Here's how to tell designer camp wear from the real thing:

Fit

Outdoor clothing should be cut large enough to permit unrestricted movement of arms and legs, even when extra clothing is worn beneath. Shirt and jacket sleeves should be generously sized, even to the point of "billowing."

Designer outdoor wear is almost always restrictive in the arms and chest and is usually cut on the short side. This style looks flattering but is an abomination in the wilds. A rule of thumb is that properly sized wind and rain gear should have sleeves which are twice the diameter of your arms!

Hoods: Designer hoods are slim, trim, and stow away into collars. "Wilderness" hoods are large enough to fit over a brimmed hat. Hood zippers continue to the nose. This "continuous zipper" design naturally precludes a stow away feature, essential to the designer look.

Designer wear also features more pockets than you can possibly use, which suggests utility and drives up tailoring costs. Really now, when was the last time you used more than two pockets in your parka or rain jacket?

Least expensive and most versatile trousers for camping are military surplus chinos and fatigues. For cold weather use, surplus wool trousers are the norm. Trouser legs should hang straight (no cuffs) so they won't trap the environment as you walk through it.

The U.S. army field jacket, available at every surplus store, makes a fine four-season parka, and is in fact identical to commercial "mountain parkas" which cost much more money.

Sew Velcro tabs to the hem of each trouser leg so you can seal off this area from black flies and mosquitoes.

Before you leave on a lengthy camping trip, have your cotton/polyester garments dry cleaned and "waterproofed" at any drycleaning establishment. Drycleaners apply "Scotchguard" (or similar compound) which slightly stiffens the fabric but makes it quite water resistant (not waterproof). You can do the job yourself with an aerosol can of "Scotchguard" or "Thompson's Sport Seal," but the result will be quite inferior to that of a professional drycleaner. And, the cost will be about the same.

Despite the ballyhoo over new synthetic fabrics like polypropylene, pile, and chemically treated dacrons, good wool performs about as well in cold damp weather. In practice, the human body is less sensitive than the machines used to prove manufacturers' claims of superiority. Buy what you can afford but don't be swept off your feet by exotic claims for space-age fabrics. Only cotton, in pure form is unsuitable for serious camping.

Blue jeans are a particularly bad choice and have accounted for several deaths due to hypothermia. Even in the July heat of summer, there are better choices than "pure cotton."

Tip: Pack a small nylon sack inside your clothes bag or pack. This "dirty laundry bag" will keep dirty clothing separate from clean items.

Care and Cleaning of Clothing

Woolens may be drycleaned or washed by hand or machine (gentle cycle only). Best method is to hand wash — three minute soak in a mild detergent (Woolite, Ivory Snow, or any mild dishwashing detergent), then hand-rinse and spin-dry in a machine.

Spun-dry woolens are best dried on wooden hangers, out of direct sunlight.

To alter the fit of wool garments: Everyone knows that woolens shrink when exposed to hot water and rough handling. However, shrunken garments can also be restored to a semblance of their original shape by re-washing, stretching, and slow drying. These unique characteristics of wool will enable you to get a custom fit from military surplus and garage sale items.

For example, the sleeves on most shirts are too long for me so I shrink them by washing them (just the sleeves) in *very hot* water. The shirt is then spun dry in a hot clothes dryer. Careful monitoring of the drying process produces the exact sleeve length I want. When sleeves have shrunk, they'll hold their size for the lifetime of the garment. This procedure is not unique: For years, lobster fishermen have "boiled" their wool mittens to make them warmer and more resistant to wind. This is the same principal used in the manufacture of world famous Dachstein mittens and sweaters. Wool hats, gloves — anything can be made more wind and water-proof by "boiling."

Polypropylene garments cannot be dry-cleaned. The solvent will dissolve the plastic fibers. Hand or machine wash in cold water and air dry. Polypropylene melts at very low temperatures, so don't ever place these garments in a hot clothes dryer or too near a fire.

Polypropylene accumulates body oils and smells quite ripe after a few days of hard use. Embedded grime also reduces the thermal efficiency of the fibers, so wash these garments frequently. Because of their tendency to retain odors, hunters are switching from polypropylene underwear back to traditional woolens. Deer can probably smell a sweaty polypro undershirt a mile away when the wind is right!

Gore-Tex must be washed frequently to maintain waterproof-ness. "Ivory Snow" was the recommended soap for early Gore-Tex garments; now any good powdered detergent can be used. Wash in *cold* water and rinse thoroughly — you must get all the detergent out! Better yet, use one of the efficient, complete-rinsing Gore-Tex cleansers sold at camping shops. Air or tumble-dry Gore-Tex products at *low* heat. *Do not* dry-clean Gore-Tex items; you'll destroy them beyond repair!

Coated fabrics (rain gear) must never be dry-cleaned or machine washed. Hand wash them in warm water with any good detergent. Rinse and air dry.

Be sure coated fabrics are *bone dry* before you store them away. The stitching and nylon won't rot but the polyurethane coat-ings will. Certain microorganisms attack polyurethane coatings, which will cause separation (peeling) of the chemical from the fabric.

Compass

Background: The most practical and reliable field compass is the Silva system Orienteering type. This compass features a built-in protractor which allows you to compute bearings *without* orienting the map to north, and a liquid damped needle which stops in three seconds. Detailed instructions come with all Orienteering compasses. However, you should know how to determine *declination*.

Declination is the angular difference between geographic or true north and the direction the compass needle points. As you can see from the standard declination diagram below (Figure C-7), the difference can be quite large, especially if you live in the far east or west. Precise declination information (to the nearest fraction of a degree) is given in the legend of all topographic maps.

To adjust your compass for declination, apply the rhyme: DECLINATION EAST, COMPASS LEAST ... OR DECLINATION WEST, COMPASS BEST.

Example: You are traveling in California where the declination, as given in the diagram (and your topo map sheet) is 16 degrees

Figure C-7. Standard declination diagram.

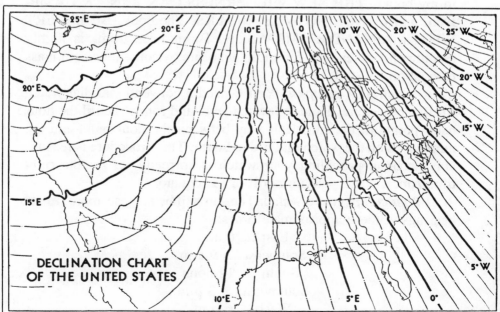

east. You have computed a *true* map heading to an objective, using the protractor function of your Orienteering compass. Your true map heading is due east, or 90 degrees. Adjust this figure for declination by applying the EAST IS LEAST (subtract) rhyme: Simply subtract 16 degrees from 90 degrees and travel on a magnetic heading of 74 degrees.

Conversely, the declination would be added (WEST IS BEST) to your map bearing if you lived in New York, east of the zero (agonic) declination line.

Note: It makes no difference in which cardinal direction you are traveling on your map sheet. The declination in your area holds constant for the entire map sheet (usually), and there is seldom more than a few degrees of difference from one area of a state to another. Once you have determined your area declination you need only remember the rhyme to apply it to any true direction computed from your map.

One degree of compass error equals approximately 92 feet per mile of ground error, so you must consider declination when traveling in regions substantially distant from the agonic line.

A detailed discussion of the compass and its use will be found in my books, THE NEW WILDERNESS CANOEING & CAMPING, and CANOEING WILD RIVERS. The book, BE EXPERT WITH MAP AND COMPASS, by Bjorn Kjellstrom, is highly recommended reading for those who are serious about compass navigation.

Your watch as a compass: You'll need a conventional dial watch for this procedure. Hold the watch level and rotate it until the hour hand points to the sun. Half way between the hour hand and the number 12 on the watch dial is due South. This procedure is reasonably accurate providing your watch is correctly set for the right time zone ... and you are north of the equator.

Your compass as a watch: The sun will be at these approximate bearings at these approximate times:

East ... 6 a.m.

Southeast ... 9 a.m.

South ... 12 noon

Southwest ... 3 p.m.

West ... 6 p.m.

Contact Cement

Best adhesive to use for gluing fabrics and/or porous items. Useful applications include patching holes in canvas tents and bags, gluing foam knee pads into canoes, repairing holes and tears in nylon fabrics, etc. *Weldwood* contact cement, in my experience, is the most reliable.

Cooking and Food Ideas
(See BAKING, also)

Cookware: Prepackaged "Trail King" cooksets are a waste of money. Pot sizes are usually awkward and the frying pans are awful. Experienced campers usually assemble their own cookware, buying only those items which they need. For a crew of eight, you'll need:

a)   *Three nesting aluminum pots,* the largest of which is 20 cups. Best camping pots are those made by Sigg of Switzerland. Next best are American made "Mirro." Choose low-sided broad pots rather than high narrow ones. A low center-of-gravity is important if you're cooking on a less than rock-stable trail stove.

b)   *Coffee pot:* An eight cup aluminum pot is ideal for a crew of four. A 20 cup model is more suitable for groups of eight or more. Coffee pots are ordinarily left on the fire as a major supply of boiling water, so consider the merits of an oversize (20 cup) pot, even for small groups. A large coffee pot will speed heating of dishwater.

c)   *Skillet:* A ten inch diameter teflon-lined skillet is all you need. Remove the bakelite handle and substitute a captive screw and wing-nut for the wrench-tightened system provided. Or, leave off the handle and use an aluminum pliers or "pot lifter." The handle must be removable so your skillet will nest with your cookset. For large groups, include a twelve inch square teflon griddle.

Store your cookset in a nylon bag.

Utensils: Experienced campers carry only an insulated plastic cup, metal spoon, and sturdy plastic bowl. The individual belt or pocket knife performs all cutting chores. Forks — useful for vehicle camping — are considered a luxury. It's best to have identical, colored, nesting bowls. Keep bowls in a fabric bag, stored inside your smallest cookpot.

You'll need these cooking utensils:

a)   plastic pancake turner

b)   rubber spatula, for scraping uneaten food from pots and bowls.

c)   wood stirring spoon.

d)   aluminum pliers or "pot grabber."

e)   small wire whip for reconstituting instant mixes.

f)   salt, pepper and other spices are best stored in plastic 35 mm film cans.

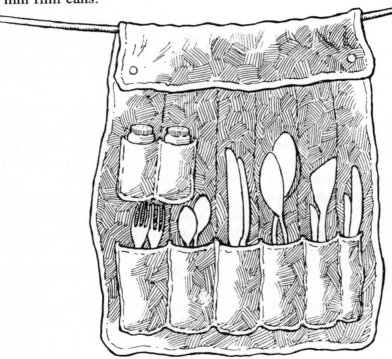

Figure C-8. Fabric utensil roll.

Fabric utensil roll (Fig. C-8) to store tools and spices. Set snaps or Velcro tabs at the top (as illustrated) so you can hang the roll from a tight line, out-of-contact with wet ground. If you string a tight rope under your rain tarp (see RAIN TARP, page 87) and hang your utensil roll from it, everything will remain dry in the rain.

Coffee pots are commonly used on open fires and so get quite black outside. Don't wash coffee pot exteriors; instead, stow the pot in a plastic-lined nylon sack between uses.

Drying dishes: Pack a half dozen sheets of paper toweling with each meal you pack. The toweling is convenient for drying cookware, cleaning the stove, etc.

For a gourmet treat, drop chunks of raw fish into boiling soup and cook for a maximum of five minutes. Sounds terrible but tastes superb and is the logical solution to preparing fish when vegetable oil or stove fuel is in short supply.

Making popcorn: If you're tired of trying to season popcorn in a pot that's too small, try this: Carry some large grocery sacks on your next campout. As you complete each batch of popcorn, pour the corn into the paper bag (don't use a plastic bag — hot popcorn will melt right through it). Season the corn and shake the bag to mix. When the popcorn's gone, burn the bag ... or fold and store it in a plastic bag for future use.

Making biscuits and cakes: Mix batter in a plastic zip-lock bag. Add the water you need, knead the bag with your hands until the consistency of the mix is correct, then punch a hole in the bag bottom and force the gooey mess into your awaiting oven. Burn the plastic bag. No mess or fuss.

Quick 'n easy trail suppers can be prepared by adding any or all of these items to boiling soup mix: instant rice, dry noodles, elbow macaroni, Bisquick dumplings (use a plastic bag to mix), potato buds.

Pasta for lunch: Bagels (a traditionally Jewish food) are ideal trail bread. Buy the frozen kind, which will keep nicely for about a week after thawing. Pile bagels high with sausage, cheese, peanut butter and jelly for a nutritious lunch. Bagels are tasty, tough, and they pack well.

Pita (Mediterranean pocket bread) is another alternative to trail crackers. Pita contains preservatives (bagels do not) and will remain fresh and tasty for at least two weeks in typical summer weather. One pita bread per person is substantial lunch fare, when combined with the usual noon time extras.

Cheese in soup? You bet! Sprinkle dried Parmesan cheese on soup for a gourmet treat. Chunks of cheese (any kind) add spark, flavor, and calories to trail spaghetti and chili.

Peanut butter on pancakes? Sounds awful but tastes divine. The peanut butter melts into the hotcakes and provides a rich taste.

To make good tasting boiled camp coffee: Bring water to a rolling boil, then remove the pot from heat. Add one tablespoon of ground coffee per cup, plus an extra tablespoon for the pot. Stir coffee into the water, put on a lid, and set the pot aside for five minutes to allow the grounds to settle. *Do not* boil pot-brewed camp coffee; you'll destroy the delicate flavor and introduce a muddy metallic taste.

For classy coffee, add cinnamon or almond extract to your camp coffee and you'll draw raves from everyone. A quarter teaspoon of almond extract or powdered cinnamon per eight cups of coffee is about right.

To make delicious camp "mocha," use one packet of hot-chocolate mix per cup. Fill cup with fresh-brewed coffee and top with some mini-marshmallows. Teenagers love this drink!

Hot pancakes for a big crew: Mix pancake syrup and margarine or butter in a small pot and heat to near boiling. This will assure pancakes are really hot when they are prepared in advance for a large group.

A Thermos bottle is a practical accessory, even on strenuous hiking trips. Boiling water poured into a vacuum bottle that is not used for beverages may provide the nucleus for hot dishwater later. Saves running the stove (using precious gas) to heat dishwater.

Pre-packaging saves time! Pre-pack everything you need to prepare a given meal, in a zip-lock plastic bag. Everything should be pre-measured and mixed so that you don't have to fuss with this on the trail. For added security, I traditionally pack my plastic-bagged breakfasts in *green* nylon bags, my lunches in *blue*, and my suppers in *red*. This saves considerable pack-groping at meal times and provides abrasion resistance for the tear-prone zip-locks inside. Adhesive tape labels identify the specific contents of each nylon bag.

How to prepare freeze-dried foods so they always taste good!

Background: Freeze-dried foods are fickle. Prepare 'em according to directions one day and they're great. Repeat the procedure another time and ... ugh!

Take heart. Here's a foolproof cooking method that works regardless of the weather, the Zodiac, or a cranky stove.

Step One

Read the cooking directions but don't take them too seriously. What works at home on the range often fails on a flat rock in a norwester.

Step Two

Separate the component parts of the food. Generally, there are two parts — a meat portion, and a noodle, rice or vegetable portion. Sometimes a third "spice packet" is included. (See Note #1 at the end of this procedure for the specifics of preparing cook-in-the-bag meals like those made by "Mountain House.")

Typical directions say: Add contents of all packets to X cups of boiling water. Reduce heat, simmer 15-20 minutes or until noodles (or whatever) are tender.

Step Three

Put 20 percent *more* water in your cooking pot than the directions call for, and add the meat portion only to the *cold* water. Bring the water to a boil and add a healthy dash of "All-Spice" (suggested recipe below):

Mix approximately equal amounts of the following spices:
Oregano
Dash of onion powder
Marjoram
Dash of thyme
Seasoned salt and pepper mixture (I buy a commercial blend.)

Step Four

When the water is at a rolling boil, add contents of the spice packet (if there is one). Reduce heat to slow boil and let spices and meat stew together for a full five minutes. If there is no spice packet allow meat to stew for five minutes before you proceed to step five.

Step Five

Add contents of noodle, rice or vegetable packet to the boiling water. Reduce heat, cover, simmer and stir occasionally for the amount of time indicated in the package directions.

Step Six

Eat and enjoy. All portions of the meal are thoroughly cooked and the taste has been fully developed.

Notes: Why some meals fail

1.   You haven't cooked the meat long enough. Half-cooked reconstituted meat spoils the whole stew. Except in very warm weather, "cook-in-the-bag" foods just don't get done. It's best to place the cooking bag in a covered pot of near boiling water for 10 minutes. Add about 10 percent more water to the cooking bag than the directions call for.

2.   You burned the pasta! This is easy to do on a one-burner trail stove, especially if you plop the contents of all food packets into the boiling water simultaneously. If your stove's turned high, you may burn the meal quicker than you can say "turn the heat down, Jack!"

3.   Insufficient water. Remember, you can always boil out too much water, but there's not much you can do with a stew that's so thick it's burned and glued to the pot bottom.

4.   Not enough spices. Don't underestimate the value of spices when preparing freeze-dried foods. Most quick-cook products are unacceptably bland unless they're well spiced. The suggested "All-Spice" works wonders on everything from spaghetti to shrimp-creole.

5.   Spoilage: Dehydrated foods come packed in plastic and have a shelf life of about one year. This is because plastic is not a complete water barrier. Freeze-dried foods come packaged in aluminum foil, which is an absolute vapor barrier. Consequently, these products have an unlimited shelf life.

This should tell you something about end-of-season food sales. Don't buy dehydrated foods in September if you plan to use them the following July. Your autumn "bargain" may turn out to be summer indigestion.

It's important to realize that many products contain both freeze-dried and dehydrated components (for example, spaghetti with freeze-dried meatballs). While the foil-wrapped meatballs won't spoil, the plastic wrapped spaghetti and spices might. Only foods which are *completely* sealed in foil are immune to spoilage. Unfortunately, you almost never see these products offered at sale prices.

6.   Introduction of bacteria and/or water vapor during repackaging. Don't handle dried foods or expose them to air any longer

than necessary when you repackage them. This will reduce the chance of bacteria and water vapor getting into the food.

Slice meat and cheese with a knife that's been dipped in boiling water for a full minute. This will also reduce transfer of bacteria into the food.

Blacken your pot bottoms: Some campers meticulously scrub and brighten their cooking pots after use, but fire-blackened pots heat faster and more evenly. *Aluma-black*, a chemical used to blacken aluminum gun sights and mounts, works wonders on pot bottoms. Just daub the chemical on the pot, allow it to dry, and a rich blue-black color will result. Aluma-black is available from most gun shops. It is quite inexpensive. The product may also be used to darken the decks and rails of aluminum canoes and fishing boats.

Cold weather cooking tips

Stoves used on snow must be set on a support of some sort or they'll melt the snow beneath and quietly sink out of sight. Fires built in snow must also have a suitable support.

Don't set stoves on pieces of closed cell foam (so the fuel tank will retain heat ... and pressure) as is recommended by some authorities. A hot stove will melt the foam and stick solidly to it.

Pot covers are essential for winter cooking. Open pots lose too much heat; in sub-zero temperatures, water may not reach boiling unless it is placed in a covered pot.

Snow provides a natural windscreen. Dig in your stove so it's completely protected from wind. Sub-zero temps and a good wind will lengthen cooking times considerably.

Insulate your water bottles so they won't freeze: Carry water bottles in an inside parka pocket so they won't freeze. In camp, store them *upside down* in the snow. The frozen interface will then be at the bottom and you'll be able to pour the liquid from the capped end. Snow is a marvelous insulator: Water bottles stored overnight this way will be "pourable" come morning.

Light for the kitchen: Winter days come early; often there is insufficient light to cook by. Traditional flashlights lose power in cold weather and are awkward to hold. Select instead a powerful headlamp (one that will accept alkaline D-size batteries). Keep the battery pack *inside* your parka when the light is used.

Securing drinking water in winter may require that you bore through the ice of a frozen lake. For this, an ice chisel is better than the traditional cumbersome auger. Fit a short length of threaded pipe to the tail of the chisel so you can screw on a pole to provide weight when chopping. Don't use a handaxe for chiseling; it is awkward and dangerous.

How to wash dishes in sub-freezing temperatures: Heavy rubber gloves will protect hands from the wet chilling effects of cold. Dish water should be near boiling. A copper sponge or 3M nylon pad is all you need to remove food particles from pots and bowls. Detergents aren't necessary as there is no bacterial growth in subfreezing temperatures. In fact, dishes need not be washed at all. Some authorities recommend that you clean dishes with snow — a particularly inefficient practice. Boiling water and rubber gloves work much better!

Foods that don't work well in winter: Frozen cheese looks and tastes like candle tallow. Peanut butter and jelly are sure to be frozen; there is no way to keep these items thawed unless you carry them in your pockets.

Gasoline is dangerous in cold weather! Gasoline, naptha (Coleman fuel), and kerosine freeze at very low temperature. If these fuels contact exposed skin in sub-zero temperatures, instant frostbite will result. Always wear rubber gloves when fueling stoves in cold weather. (See *Stoves,* page 109, for a thorough discussion of safety and trouble-shooting procedures.)

Cord
(see ROPE, for knots and hitches)

Best camp utility cord is one-eighth inch diameter nylon parachute cord. Nylon cord should be "hot cut" (use a butane lighter) rather than sliced, so its core and sheath won't separate.

Singe (melt) the ends of nylon and polypropylene cord and rope to prevent them from unravelling. Nobody "whips" ropes anymore.

Nylon cord-locks, which are available at all camp shops are handy for securing the chute-cord thongs of nylon sacks. A less

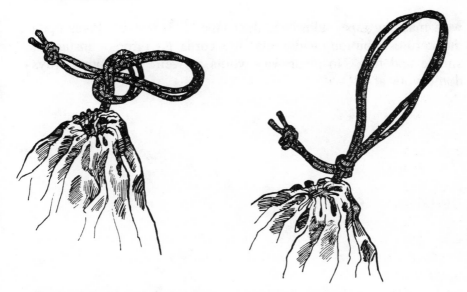

Figure C-9. Secure your stuff sack with a quick-release loop.

expensive solution that works as well is to purchase nylon hose clamps from scientific supply houses. You can buy a dozen rubber hose (tubing) clamps for the price of one "cord-lock."

You don't need cord-locks to secure the thongs of nylon stuff sacks if you learn the simple knot illustrated in Figure C-9.

Cord Locks

Cordlocks are small, spring-loaded nylon clamps which are used to secure the cords of sleeping bags, parka hoods and stuff sacks. Every camping shop carries a goodly supply of them for the do-it-yourselfer who wants to add versatility to his/her camping outfit.

Now comes the hard part — threading the pair of one-eighth inch diameter nylon parachute cords through the tiny cordlock hole. One cord goes through easily; the second dies a slow death in mid-push. Ultimately frustration reigns and the "good idea" is disgustingly thrown into a drawer for use later.

Here's an easy way to thread the paired cords through the cordlock hole: Place the tips of the cords side by side, one tip one-eighth inch below the other. Then tape the two tightly together with masking tape, adhesive, duct tape ... whatever. Press open the cordlock button, and voila, the cords go through instantly, simple and fast. No other way works as well. Most other ways don't work at all!

— D —

Diapers (cloth) make the best camp towels. They're lightweight, compact and absorbent.

Duct tape is the most useful repair item you can have. The hard-to-find olive-drab "army" tape sticks better than the common gray tape found in hardware stores. 3-M brand sliver duct tape is the best!

Ethics

-The imperfect science of sanitation and ethical camping proce-dures-

Background: It is no longer acceptable to build beds of green pine boughs (or dead ones, for that matter), lash log furniture, trench tents, hack green trees and otherwise disturb the natural environment to suit our whims. There's just too little of the wilderness and too many of us. If we are to preserve the remaining backcountry for future generations, then each of us must adopt a solemn "I care" attitude. We must unfailingly practice ethical use of our natural resources, and we must teach — indeed, preach — ethics to all who will listen. And for those who turn the other ear, there must be laws ... and penalties. The alternative is regulation upon regulation and a lessened quality of experience for everyone. Here are the recommended land and water use procedures:

Disposal of human and food wastes: Bury these wastes in mineral soil (if possible), four to twelve inches deep. The upper foot of soil contains the majority of decomposer organisms and so ensures the fastest rate of decay.

Toilet paper should be burned. Unburned tissue may take a

season or more to degrade. Human waste will be gone in a matter of days if the weather is warm. When camping on the granite rock of the Canadian shield, or anywhere soil cover is at a premium, simply follow the recommended procedure for "shallow burial" and cover the waste with whatever soil cover is available.

Please do not leave leftover food around camp "for the animals" — this will upset their ecology and make them dependent on man, not to mention the aggravation they'll bestow on campers who will later occupy the site.

Fish entrails: It is illegal in most states to throw fish entrails into a lake or river, and for good reason. Bacteria consume the viscera and multiply, which raises germ levels to possibly dangerous proportions. Bacteria also use vast amounts of oxygen, which in turn robs fish and aquatic organisms of this essential element. Since food scraps react similarly, they too should never be tossed into a body of water.

Bury fish remains as you would food wastes — 100 feet from water and well away from the campsite area. If you are camping in a very remote area where seagulls are common, you may leave viscera on a large rock — well away from human habitation — for the gulls. This procedure *is not* acceptable on heavily used lakes!

Cans and bottles should always be packed out of the wilderness. Tin cans should be burned out and crushed flat with the back of an axe or your boot, then packed out. The typical steel can requires about 75 years to decompose completely; aluminum cans may need 500 years! A glass bottle could last one million years in the environment! We do not bury cans and bottles today. We PACK THEM OUT!

Your garbage detail will be easier if you make a strong nylon bag, with drawstring, for this purpose.

Dish washing: Dishes should never be washed in a waterway. Food scraps encourage bacterial growth and even biodegradable detergents kill essential microorganisms. Dishes should be washed *on land* in a large cooking pot. Dish water is best disposed of on mineral soil, 100 feet from a lake or river.

Swimming is fine, but "bathing" is not. If you use soap to wash your hair and body, please rinse on the shore (with a bucket of water), well away from the water's edge.

And a word about biodegradable products: It's fashionable today to extol the virtues of biodegradable products over those which do not break down by bacterial action. Certainly, you should choose biodegradable detergents, tissues, and toilet paper whenever possible. Be aware, however, that even the best biodegradable products depend upon bacteria, moisture ... and time for decomposition. And this means increased germ counts, lowered levels of oxygen, and visual pollution for some time. There's no such thing as a free ride!

Bough beds: Cutting evergreen branches to make bough beds is illegal, immoral, and damaging to the trees. An air mattress or foam pad works better. The use of *dead* evergreen boughs or mosses should also be discouraged as this material provides a "surface cover" which blots out sunlight and consequently kills vegetation below. Campsites should always be left as natural as possible so that nature can effectively do "its thing."

Cutting green trees is, of course, illegal and damaging. Since green wood burns poorly, there's no sense cutting it for firewood. You'll find plenty of good dead fire wood in the backcountry if you look for it (see FIRE MAKING, page 46).

Graffitti: It's always shocking to see initials and names carved or painted on trees and rocks in the backcountry. But it does happen, even in the most remote wilderness. The rationale is certainly ignorance and insensitivity, neither of which can be tolerated by those of us who know and care.

Noise: Most people take to the backcountry to experience peace and quiet. Loud, man-made disturbances are obviously unwelcome, and in state and national parks, usually illegal. Please keep radios at home or use a personal "Walkman."

Color: Some campers are offended by brightly colored camping gear and clothing. Consequently, the trend is toward gentle "earth tones" — greens, browns and grays. However, there's no denying the safety (and photographic) advantages of brightly colored tents, canoes and clothing in remote areas. Despite much hoopla, the color issue is over-exaggerated. There are more pressing environmental concerns in the backcountry.

Lugged hiking boots: Chunky soled mountain boots churn up much more soil than non-aggressive footwear and are therefore discouraged in popular hiking areas. Primitive peoples got along quite nicely without Vibram lugs and you will too, not to mention the freedom of foot you'll enjoy by selecting lighter more flexible shoes. Nonetheless, the damage that results from use of Rambo-style boots is probably over-rated. Like "color," there are more pressing concerns.

Fire site: Fire sites should always be left as natural as possible. In military terms, "everything that's not growing or nailed down" should be removed from the premises. Every scrap of paper, every shred of aluminum foil, down to the tiniest speck, should be picked out and hauled home. Ideally, there should be no partially burned wood left in the grate — absolutely everything should be consumed by flame before you pass on.

It is permissible, but no longer traditional (or even desirable) to leave cut firewood for those who will later occupy the site. Some modern campers consider the sight of a woodpile an "affront," one which detracts from the wildness of the area. So cut only the wood you need and put your fire dead out — check it with your hands to be sure it is DEAD OUT! — before you leave.

Education: Unfortunately, there are not yet enough of us who care who will carry the banner for ethical land use. We must spread the word as gospel, but quietly, sensibly and in a non-intimidating way, with full realization that you can always get more bears with honey than with guns. Studies show that the majority of campers mean well even though they often do what is improper. Most abuse occurs out of ignorance. The majority of people will willingly follow your lead if properly taught.

Fire-Making Procedures

Background: Anyone can start a fire on a bone-dry day, or when they're armed with dry newspaper, kerosine or charcoal lighter. But let the day deteriorate to persistent rain, and where there's smoke there won't be fire!

Here's how to make and maintain fire when foul weather comes to stay:

Tools: You'll need a sharp knife, handaxe, and a saw (folding saws are highly recommended). Contrary to the ravings of some "authorities," it is nearly impossible to make fire in prolonged rain without *all* these tools.

Procedure

1. In an evergreen forest: Collect several handfuls of the *dead lower* branches of evergreen trees (commonly termed "squaw wood"). Wood should grade in size from pencil-lead thickness to no bigger than your little finger, and it should break with a crisp, audible snap. If you don't hear the positive "snap," the wood is too wet, in which case proceed directly to step 3.

If "squaw-wood" is suitably dry, it will burst into a bright flame the moment a match is applied. Use a small candle to provide sustained heat to your tinder ball if the bark of the squaw-wood is wet. From this point on, it's simply a matter of adding more wood and protecting the developing blaze from rain (see *To maintain fire in a driving rain*).

2. Look for resin blisters on the outside bark of balsam fir trees. Break a few blisters with a sharp stick and collect the highly volatile resin. Use the resin as a "chemical fire-starter" to propel your tinder to flame.

3. Locate a *dead, downed* tree and saw off a portion which does not touch the ground. Grounded wood rots quickly, so is apt to be unsound. Especially search for deadfalls which overhang into a sun-lit clearing or waterway. These are almost certain to be rot-free, as sunlight kills microorganisms which cause decay.

If you cannot find a dead downed tree to saw up, look for any floating log. If the log "floats," the center is dry. Splittings taken from the heart will burn.

4. When you have completed your first saw cut through the deadfall, check the center of the cut log with your hand. Is it bone dry? It should be. Even a month long rain will seldom soak through a six inch log!

5. Saw the deadfall into 12 inch sections then split each chunk with your handaxe by the method illustrated in Figure A-1. It should require only a few minutes to reduce each log chunk to half-inch diameter kindling by this procedure.

6. Cut wafer-thin tinder from a few splittings with your pocket knife. The key to producing long thin shavings rather than little squiggly ones is to use a sawing, rather than whittling action with your knife. Even a small dull knife will produce nice shavings if you persistently saw the blade back and forth.

7. Build a well-ventilated platform fire according to Steps 1,2,3.

Step One

Establish a fire base of one inch diameter sticks as illustrated. Place pencil-thin "support" sticks at right angles to the fire base.

Step Two

Meticulously stack wafer-thin shavings on top of the kindling to a height of about one inch. Place the shavings so that plenty of

Figure F-1. Fire building procedures: Step 1.

Pencil-thin kindling

6"

One-inch thick sticks

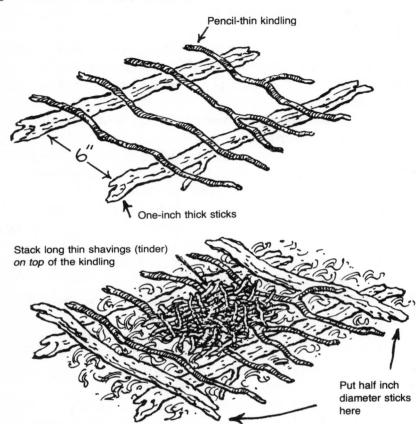

Stack long thin shavings (tinder)
on top of the kindling

Put half inch
diameter sticks
here

Figure F-2. Fire building procedures: Step 2.

Add fine split kindling above the tinder
box to lock the tinder in place.

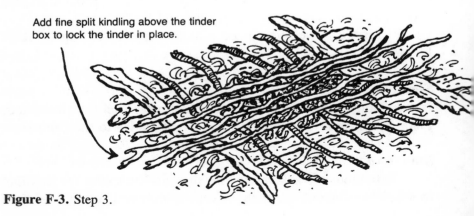

Figure F-3. Step 3.

air can get between them. "Smoke" is nature's way of saying you're smothering the flame!

Next, put two half inch diameter "support" sticks at right angles to the fire base. These will support the heavier kindling you'll add over the tinder in step 3.

Step Three

Now, pile on fine split kindling above the tinder box to lock the tinder in place. Again, leave space between the splittings so your fire can "breathe."

Your fire is now ready to light. Apply flame directly below the tinder (shavings). A small candle will furnish the sustained heat necessary to ignite damp wood.

Hand feed shavings (not kindling) one at a time into the developing flame. Don't heap kindling on until you have a bright reliable blaze.

Hints: Carry strike anywhere matches in addition to a butane lighter and candle. Keep matches in a plastic jar with a cotton wad on top. A spent 16 gauge shotshell nested inside a 12 gauge case makes a tough watertight match safe.

Some campers waterproof matches by painting on nail polish, but this causes match heads to deteriorate. A waterproof match case is a better idea.

An effective method of drying matches is to draw them briskly though your hair. Don't use your clothes; they are too abrasive.

"Fire-Ribbon" — a semi-liquid fire-starting paste is available at most camp stores. Just squeeze it on like toothpaste. A summer's supply will fit in a 35 mm film can.

You can make your own fire-starters by soaking miniature "logs" of rolled newspaper in paraffin.

Cotton balls dipped in Vaseline make wonderful fire-starters!

Emergency fire-making kits: You'll need a flattened half gallon milk carton, a handful of wood shavings (cedar is best), some splittings of scrap wood, fire-ribbon, and a small candle. Store everything in a Zip-lock bag. When the emergency strikes, frizz up the milk carton, splash tinder with Fire- Ribbon, and light your match. Materials will burn reliably for at least five minutes — enough time for you to search the woods for additional fuel.

"Pitch pine" Highly volatile resins (pitch) are commonly stored in the roots of evergreen trees. Splittings taken from dead stumps

will burn vigorously, even in driving rain. Look for "pitch pine" in areas which have been recently logged or burned.

Witch's broom is a blue-gray lichen which grows on the branches of some evergreen trees. It is extremely flammable when dry.

Paper is hydrophyllic (loves water). It absorbs moisture on damp days. Don't depend on paper to start your fires!

In an emergency, you can always burn money!

One or two sticks robbed from a beaver's house makes good kindling and tinder. Beaver wood has been "de-barked" so it is apt to be rot-free. For the sake of the beaver, please take only one or two sticks, then, only in an emergency.

Emergency ignitors: You can't beat a butane lighter and dry matches! The chemically impregnated magnesium rods sold as "survival tools" will ignite *dry* tinder, but are next to worthless when things are damp. And magnifying glasses must be very large (at least two inches in diameter) to reliably ignite tinder.

Steel wool makes excellent emergency tinder.

Flour (any kind) will burst into potent flames if sprinkled lightly over a blaze.

Cooking oil (vegetable oil) will enrich a flame only if the fire is already very hot.

An unused rain jacket or small square of plastic will provide all the overhead protection you need to start a fire in a driving rain. And so will an overturned canoe, propped up by paddles shoved through the seat braces.

To maintain fire in a driving rain: Build a loose "log cabin" around your fire with whatever wood is available. Construct a two tier, flat "roof" for your cabin from newly cut kindling and fuel. The "roof" will deflect rain and the fire below will dry out the lower level of wood and bring it to flame. If you maintain a two tier roof, you'll have a continuous supply of dry wood no matter how much it rains. Note: since you're robbing the fire of oxygen, expect smoke...lots of it!

Banking the fire to preserve fuel: Use this procedure when you have a good hot fire but little wood to maintain it.

"Bank" your fire by setting small logs, parallel to one another, across the top. Rule-of-thumb for a smoke-free flame is to allow a "radius width" between parallel pieces of wood. Thus, a pair of two-inch thick logs should be separated by a full inch to ensure adequate ventilation. "Banking" will reduce this distance to a mere (though identifiable) slit, which will naturally diminish use of oxygen and slow combustion. You should also shut off any breeze coming into the fire. A large flat rock or a tier of logs will work fine.

Extinguishing the fire: Throwing water on a fire is not good enough. You must ascertain it is out by checking the fire bed with your hands. If water is in short supply, use the "stir/sprinkle/stir" method outlined below.

1.   Sprinkle a handful of water on the flames with your hands. Continue to sprinkle until the fire has gone out.

2.   Stir the fire with a stick and sprinkle some more. Repeat as needed until the fire is DEAD OUT!

First-Aid: The Common Ailments

The following tips and procedures are from the pen of my friend Dr. Tom Schwinghamer. Tom is a family practitioner, an emergency room physician and CEO of River Valley Clinic in Hastings, Minnesota. Before coming to Hastings, Tom practiced general medicine for 10 years in the U.S./Canadian border town of Ely, Minnesota. Here, he again and again came to grips with the injuries and ailments unique to the Boundary Waters Canoe Area wilderness environment. Tom took the job of doctoring so seriously that for a time he owned a small airplane which he used to reach and evacuate injured victims.

I've had the good fortune to canoe many remote wilderness rivers with Tom Schwinghamer and to watch his expertise at work. His state-of-the-art methods and medications are uniquely tempered by the essential practicalities imposed by rugged, non-sterile wilderness settings and, by the experience of one who has often treated life-threatening injuries alone without exotic hospital equipment. (CJ)

Says Tom Schwinghamer, "Most of the wilderness accidents I encountered in Ely were self-inflicted — mostly drownings, frostbite and falls — that resulted from poor planning and careless behavior. Pre-trip planning that emphasizes caution is the best medical kit you can carry. There are no simple solutions for drownings, head injuries or multiple fractures. For starters, a medical history on everyone in your crew is a must. You must be aware of back problems, insect sting and drug allergies, diabetes and asthma. There is simply no substitute for anticipating the unexpected. And, for being appropriately prepared!"

In preparing this section, I kept uppermost in mind that:

1.   Most wilderness travelers have little, if any, in-depth first-aid knowledge and have neither the time nor inclination to make a study of the subject. Consequently, any formula for "wilderness medicine" must be brief, easy to administer, and correct.

2.   Sanitary facilities are not available in the backcountry. Nonetheless, sanitary procedures are often essential. Outdoorspeople need some "quick 'n dirty ways" to deal effectively with this problem.

3.   Most outdoors men and women don't want to carry a sophisticated first aid kit. Medications and materials should be few, and they should fit easily into a small nylon dop kit.

4.   Most first-aid courses teach too much, in too much depth, too fast. And what is taught is seldom applicable to the wilderness environment. The majority of outdoor folk will do better to eliminate from concern heavy duty injuries and to instead concentrate on the most common disorders.

With this focus in mind, I offer these easy, practical methods for treating the most common wilderness ailments.

Equipment: building a simple, effective first-aid kit

You need only four medications, so leave the aspirin, Mercurochrome, eye and ear drops and Epsom salts at home.

1.   *DURICEF anti-biotic:* This is a broad-spectrum, 1000 mg (!) prescription drug that will kill most germs. Use it for an ear or eye infection, infected skin laceration, inflamed fish-hook site or sore throat. If it's hot, red and sore, it's probably infected, especially if there has been injury to the skin. DURICEF needs to be taken only once daily in the form of a one gram (1000 mg) tablet, so a 12 day supply will fit nicely in a 35 mm film can. DURICEF is relatively new and it requires a prescription, something your family physician will surely write if he/she knows how you plan to use it.

Caution: Do not take DURICEF if you are allergic to penicillin. Your family physician can recommend an alternate broad-spectrum antibiotic.

2. *TYLENOL #3:* This is a heavyduty pain-reliever with codeine. Again, it's a prescription drug. It can sometimes produce nausea and vomiting, though this is rare. Tylenol #3 works well for nearly all forms of pain. Take one to three tablets every four to six hours as need for pain.

3. *FELDENE, 20 mg:* Feldene is an anti-inflammatory prescription drug that is excellent for all "over-use" symptoms (see OVER-USE SYNDROMES on page 57). One tablet per day for swelling and pain is enough.

4. *BACITRACIN CREAM:* An over-the-counter broad-spectrum antibiotic cream that can be used for burns and other skin infections.

Equipment

XYLOCAINE (one percent): It's almost impossible to remove a deeply imbedded fish-hook without causing severe pain. Xylocaine is a safe, easy-to-use local anaesthetic which will make the procedure virtually painless (see fish-hook treatment on page 55 for details). Ask your family physician to get you a 3 cc syringe loaded with one percent Xylocaine.

AIR CAST (ankle/foot): Here's a foolproof recipe for a sprained ankle, one that will be helpful if the sprain later turns out to be a nondisplaced fracture. Air casts are compact and require only a few minutes to apply. They can be purchased from your local clinic, hospital supply center or Orthopedic house. This apparatus is a must for any serious backpacking or canoeing trip. Excellent instructions come with every air cast; you don't need a knowledge of splinting to apply it.

OVAL EYE PADS (sterile): Soft, contoured bandages used for corneal abrasions, blisters and any place you need lots of cushioning. Most drugstores carry them.

Tip: Eye pads work great for covering any wound. They're compact, soft and sterile.

MICROFOAM TAPE: Stretchy, foam-backed tape that stays put no matter how you move. Excellent for patching eyes, broken blisters and most wounds. This is a standard item in all clinics and is occasionally found in drugstores.

IDOFORM SPONGE (a hospital supply center item): Technically called a "Bactoscrub Surgical Sponge-Brush," this iodine/
detergent loaded sponge is great for scrubbing away dirt without
injuring tissue. The Povidone-Iodine solution kills germs. The
IDOFORM SPONGE is re-usable: store it in a Zip-lock bag between
uses.

NASAL STAT BALLOON (nasal hemostatic catheter kit):
Optional, but possibly life-saving item used to stop uncontrollable
nose bleeds (see NOSE BLEEDS on page 56 for details). This
product can be purchased from your local clinic or hospital supply
center.

EYE STREAM: Nothing more than four fluid ounces of sterile
water in a clever plastic squirt bottle. Use it for irrigating wounds,
flushing foreign matter from eyes, and anywhere you need a sterile,
irrigating solution. The plastic bottle dispenser remains sterile
throughout application of the water so you can use some now, save
some for another time. Eye Stream can be purchased at most phar-
macies.

ANAKIT: Severe allergic reactions are extremely rare but when
they do occur, they can present a life-threatening situation.
ANAKITS — available by prescription at any drugstore — have
specific directions on how to treat the individual who has become
ill from a bee sting.

FOUR YARDS OF SIX PLY GAUZE (need not be sterile).

Note: you can get prescriptions for all the suggested medications from your family physician. Other items mentioned here can
be purchased through your local clinic or hospital supply center,
or ordered by mail from Indiana Camp Supply, Inc., P.O. Box
211, Hobart, Indiana 46342.

The Mini-First-Aid Kit

If you're really going light and want the absolute minimum,
assemble these items: 12 tablets of DURACEF, 4 eye-patches, one
roll of microfoam tape, one tube of Bacitracin and a few bandaids.
With these, and due caution, you can handle most of the common
medical emergencies.

Ailments and injuries

Skin lacerations

Wound care: The initial treatment is the same whether the
wound is a laceration, scrape or burn. You'll need sterile eye irri-

gation (EYE STREAM) and an IDOFORM SPONGE. Clean the skin injury with the IDOFORM sponge and sterile water. Be sure you scrub out all the dirt and irrigate it away. Don't try to repair lacerations and don't terminate your trip because of them unless they are severe. Finish with a sterile dressing. One or two eye pads and microfoam tape will do the job on medium size wounds.

If the wound becomes infected (hot, red and sore) start antibiotics. One 1000 mg tablet of DURICEF each day will do the trick. Continue DURICEF for 10 days or until the soreness is gone.

Fish-hook

A Dardevle in the cheek will kill the planned trip. You must be able to treat this injury if you have fishermen along. A hook through the skin is one of the most common wilderness injuries.

Treatment: The common advice is to work the embedded barb through the skin, cut it off and extract the hook. But this won't work if the hook is embedded to the curve. You may have to back the hook out partially and re-set the angle so the tip will clear the skin rather than simply work deeper into it. In any case, you'll have a messy situation with lots of pain. Here's a painless way to extract the hook:

Start by injecting the entrance hole of the fish-hook with 1-2 ml of Xylocaine from the pre-loaded Xylocaine syringe. Then, wait several minutes for the drug to take effect and proceed to work the hook back out slowly. If you're unsuccessful, turn it through the skin, cut off the barb with a small wire cutters and turn it back. Then, treat the wound as a skin laceration.

Note: don't be scared off by the Xylocaine injection. There's no way you can mess up. The first time you extract a fish-hook "cold turkey" you'll understand why a local anaesthetic is so important! A less barbaric method of fish-hook extraction without Xylocaine suggested by Dr. Bill Forgey is illustrated in his book *Wilderness Medicine.*

Burns

About the only way you can get badly burned in the backcountry is to roll in the campfire while wearing polypropylene or nylon clothing. Or, get struck by lightning.

Treatment: Clean the burn with the IDOFORM SPONGE and

sterile water (see Skin lacerations). Cover with Bacitracin ointment and clean gauze dressings and observe daily. Start oral antibiotics (one 1000 mg DURICEF tablet each day) at the first sign of infection.

Blisters

First line of defense is to keep the blister from breaking, which means isolating it from the abrasion of the shoe. Standing operating procedure (SOP) is to cover the cell with "moleskin," an adhesive-backed flannel material available at drug stores. If you don't have moleskin, simply use a large bandage or an eye patch with microfoam tape.

If the blister breaks, treat it as a small burn (see Burns above). Two eye patches and microfoam tape will stabilize a broken blister well enough so that the victim can resume walking in reasonable comfort.

Bee sting

These usually produce just a sore red area but can be life-threatening to victims with bee-sting allergies. Following the directions in the ANAKIT can be lifesaving!

Frostbite

Treat these as burns and evacuate the victim if the frostbite is severe.

Eye injuries

Most common, is an invisible scratch to the "clear window" cornea. There is almost always a history of a mild injury such as a tree branch scrape 12-24 hours before the onset of pain.

Treatment: Patch the eye for just one day and administer Tylenol #3 pain medication. Patching is done not only to eliminate the irritating bright lights, but more important, to splint the eye to keep it from moving the injured part around under the lid. Use *two* oval eye pads plus 3M microfoam tape.

Ear ailments

Ear pain is almost always infection and it does not really matter whether it is middle or outer ear infection. Start DURICEF oral antibiotic early. Administer Tylenol #3 if pain is severe.

Nose ailments

Nose-bleed is the only common problem. Treat by having the patient blow out all clots from the nose then put direct pressure to the nose by pinching it for approximately 15 minutes just below the hard bony part. If, after four attempts, the bleeding persists, evacuate the victim immediately. The alternative is to carry a nasal stat balloon, which is shoved into the nasal cavity and inflated, according to the enclosed directions. If you use the balloon, begin antibiotics to prevent infection.

Note: I have never had to use a nasal stat balloon in the backcountry. However, it could be a lifesaving item in the event of an unstoppable nose-bleed. Contrary to popular belief, you *can* die from a nose bleed!

Throat ailments

Don't sit around the campfire and debate when to start antibiotics for a sore throat, infected tooth or pus-filled wound. Start antibiotics at the first sign of these infections. Cough, fever and chest pain mean pulmonary infection. One 1000 mg. DURICEF tablet each day will do the trick.

Back ailments

Back pain is usually just muscular sprain from over-use. Treatment consists of rest and pain medication (Tylenol #3).

Over-use syndromes

This is called many things and includes bursitis of the shoulder, tennis elbow, painful wrist syndrome and hands which "keep falling asleep" (a common canoeing malady). These problems all reflect soreness and swelling in an area that has been used a lot. Treatment is rest and an anti-inflammatory drug like FELDENE (take one 20 mg. tablet daily).

Ankle sprains

Use the *air cast*. Soaking the limb in cold water initially for 30 minutes will retard swelling. A real advantage of the air cast is that you can wear your boot over it and resume near normal walking almost immediately.

About using the air cast, nasal stat and other medical items: Excellent instructions come with all medical products. So don't be intimidated by your unfamiliarity with these products.

WARNING: Don't assume you can handle all emergencies with the few items suggested here. When serious injury threatens, your best bet is to evacuate the victim *immediately*. The items and methods outlined here are not a substitute for the skills of a competent physician and the controlled environment of a hospital.

Flashlights and Camp Lighting Devices

Any light used for camping should be waterproof and have a lanyard ring so it can be hung in a tent. Most popular flashlights are AA-cell models which feature lithium batteries and high intensity bulbs. These tiny lights burn out batteries and bulbs quickly, but are nice if you must have maximum brightness for minimum size. Most practical — and best value for the dollar — is the old twin-C or D cell standard flashlight, albeit with high impact plastic waterproof case.

Candle lanterns grow more popular each year but are more "cutesy" than functional. Batteries burn for about the same length of time as quality candles of similar weight, and artificial light is much brighter than open flame. Nonetheless, candle lanterns are "fun toys" and they add some warmth to a tent on chilly nights. They are best at home for winter camping where every calorie of heat is appreciated.

Mantle lanterns: Newest rage is the mini-size Coleman Peak I lantern which puts out nearly as much light (for half the size and weight) as its traditional big brother. Though mantle lanterns are considered essential equipment for auto camping, they are viewed as "gauche" by the self-propelled camping crowd. Mantles and glass globes are tougher than most people think, but not tough enough for strenuous canoe and horse packing trips.

Caution: Never inhale the fumes from a newly lit (previously unburned) mantle. The gasses which are released are highly poisonous!

If your lantern won't generate pressure, the leather pump gasket may be too dry (needs oil). Trail stoves also suffer from this malady. Most of the new pump gaskets are synthetic; the traditional leather models work better. Some leather stool washers (check the plumbing section of your hardware store) fit some lanterns and stoves perfectly!

Don't fill a mantle lantern more than three-fourths full of gas. You need air space to generate pressure.

Hypothermia

Background: Hypothermia (commonly called "exposure sickness") is the most common and dangerous of outdoor ailments. No one is immune to its icy grip. You can suffer hypothermia while climbing a mountain in Tibet or biking across Chicago. Dozens of people die from it each year.

Hypothermia occurs when body temperature drops below about ninety-five degrees Fahrenheit. As blood is rushed to the vital organs, chilling spreads throughout the body. This is accompanied by clumsiness, slurred speech, and loss of judgment. Coma and death may result within a few hours if body temperature is not raised.

Hypothermics usually cannot identify their problem. They will maintain (often, until death!) that they are "okay." You must observe symptoms, diagnose correctly, and treat quickly. Your friend's life may depend on it. Check these symptoms:

1. Slurred speech, stiffness of limb (difficulty in walking), an irrational view of reality. Victim acts irresponsibly — loses hat, mittens or other equipment along the trail. Loss of short term memory.
2. Victim can't walk a straight line.
3. Victim was shivering before, now shivering has stopped.

Note: *Mild* shivering is nature's way of re-warming the body. It does not indicate hypothermia. Hypothermia begins with *violent* shivering. Be aware, however, that some people — especially those who are over-tired — do not exhibit a shivering reflex. So do not rely on "shivering" to ascertain the onset of hypothermia!

Treatment:

1.   Provide shelter at once! Any place out of the wind and wet is good enough.

2.   Replace wet clothing with dry.

3.   Apply *moderate, even* heat. If a fire is available, use it. If there are several people in your party, have them loosely "hug" the victim to keep him/her as warm as possible.

Be sure the victim's head and neck are covered with warm clothing (hat, scarf, etc.).

If the victim can swallow, hot soup (or water) will re-warm spirits and insides. Do not administer stimulants like alcohol, coffee or tea.

For serious cases (where the victim is unable to walk, suffers amnesia, etc.), administer the "sandwich" treatment. This consists of stripping the victim's clothes and sandwiching him/her between two non-hypothermics. Cover the three-some with sleeping bags and clothing. Be sure to insulate everyone from the cold ground (use a foam trail pad, additional clothing, leaves, grass, branches etc.).

Hypothermics must be handled *gently:* rough-housing may initiate a heart attack!

4.   Hypothermia drains both body and spirit. Considerable rest is warranted after the danger subsides.

Knives

The primary use for any camp knife is in cooking and preparing foods. You'll slice vegetables, meat and cheese, spread jam and peanut butter, and cut your supper steak. Rambo survivalists will insist on a stiff-backed sheath knife with a blade at least six inches long, while more gentle souls will argue the merits of a pen knife. Between the two extremes are scores of expert campers who will agree that at least one knife in the camping party should meet these characteristics:

1. Enough length (four to five inches) to slice meat and cheese and to reach deep into the peanut butter can without getting gunked up.

2. A thin, flat-ground blade for effortless slicing.

Nearly all knives sold for outdoor use have blades which are too thick. One-eighth of an inch across the spine is the *maximum* thickness permissible for a utility knife, no matter how delicate the edge. Try slicing a tomato with the typical "hunting" knife and you'll see why!

Your favorite kitchen knife would probably be perfect for camp use if it had a bit less length, more backbone and better steel. In fact, the most popular knives on the frontier were the famous "Green River" models, which were nothing more than solidly built kitchen knives.

The primary camp knife may be a fixed blade or folding model. You'll pay much more for a good folder than for a sheath knife of similar length.

If your taste runs to folding knives, select a model with a three to four inch long, *thin*, preferably flat-ground blade. Despite advertising claims, knives with locking blades are no safer than those with traditional pressure springs. The only advantage of a lock-back is that it can be opened singlehanded while wearing mittens. Traditional folders require two hands to use.

Which knife for you? If you've read between the lines, you'll conclude that you need two knives for camping — a thin-ground kitchen style model for preparing foods, and a substantial multi-purpose folder of some sort. In case you're wondering, my favorite camp knife is a Gerber Shorty — a very strong (and ugly!) kitchen-style hunting knife with a four-and-one-half inch long flat-ground blade.

Sharpening: Don't ever sharpen a knife on an electric sharpener or one of those mechanical wheeled gadgets sold at supermarkets. You'll ruin the knife beyond repair!

Most sporting goods stores stock "diamond" stones (a first choice!) and medium grit "soft Arkansas" stones. If you want a razor edge, you'll need a "hard" Arkansas stone, as well.

Maintain a film of light oil on the natural stones (cutting oil, kerosine, or WD-40; use water on the diamond stones) to float away the steel particles which clog the pores of the stone and reduce its cutting efficiency. Clean the stone and blade frequently and apply new oil during the sharpening process.

Keep the back of the blade raised 15-20 degrees, and cut *into* the stone, while sharpening. A good way to maintain the proper angle is to adjust an overhead light so it casts a shadow along the back of the blade when the blade is laid flat on the stone. Raise the blade until the shadow just disappears and you'll have the recommended angle.

Exotic looking tools which clamp to the knife blade are sold for the purpose of maintaining the "proper sharpening angle." These

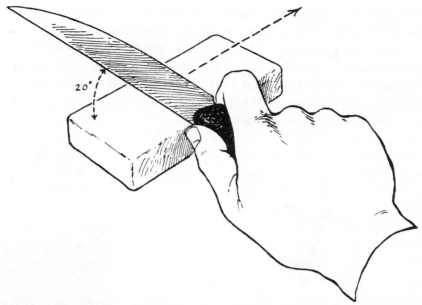

Figure K-1. Maintain a 15-20 degree angle, and cut *into* the stone. Use plenty of cutting oil and clean the stone (and blade) frequently.

tools work well but are nonetheless gimmicks for people who never learned to sharpen knives properly.

Take about four strokes per side before turning the knife over, and use plenty of oil. If you can't maintain the proper sharpening angle, try using a circular motion (not recommended) of the blade instead.

If you want a fine razor edge, complete the sharpening process on a "fine" Arkansas stone. Finish by stropping the sharpened blade (draw the blade evenly across the leather, one stroke per side) on a piece of leather impregnated with jewelers rouge.

To check for blade sharpness: A knife is considered "sharp" if it will shave hair from the back of your hand. A less barbaric method is to shine a bright light on the sharpened edge. You should see no flat spots, no inconsistencies...nothing!

Sharpening (butcher's) steels do not sharpen a knife; they merely realign the microscopic teeth of the blade edge. A steel is handy for touching up a knife (it's simply a coarse version of a leather strop) but it can't take the place of a genuine whetstone.

Tip: If you dip the blade of your knife in boiling water for about 30 seconds, it will be much easier to sharpen.

Best way to carry a hefty folding knife is in a pocket sewn into the back of your field trousers. Sew a line of stitches through the pant leg and pocket as illustrated (Fig. K-2) and attach a snap-flap or Velcro tab at the top. Equip your knife with a nylon lanyard so you can pull it out with one hand.

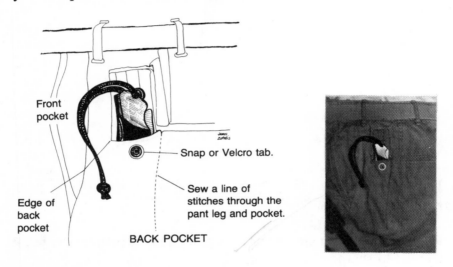

Front pocket

Snap or Velcro tab.

Sew a line of stitches through the pant leg and pocket.

Edge of back pocket

BACK POCKET

Figure K-2. Carry large folding knives in a pocket sewn into the back pocket of your field trousers.

This system is more secure, less obtrusive, and more comfortable to wear than a leather sheath worn on the belt.

To make a sheath for a fixed blade knife, you'll need: sole leather (the thicker the better), contact cement, two-piece rivets, paper, scissors, sharp utility knife. Leather and rivets may be ordered from any Tandy leather company store.

1. Make a pattern for your sheath from paper or thinly corrugated cardboard.

2. Transfer the paper pattern to the leather.

3. Soak the leather in lukewarm water until it is soft, then cut out the sheath pattern with a sharp knife.

4. Contact cement a quarter-inch wide "edge guard" of leather around the sheath perimeter.

5.   Rivet a belt loop to the back of the sheath, then contact cement the sheath edges together.

6.   Insert the knife into the glued sheath and painstakingly form the wet leather to fit. Work the hilt area carefully until you get a perfect fit.

7.   Withdraw the knife from the sheath (the leather will remain formed) and rivet — or ask your shoemaker to sew — the sheath together.

8.   When the sheath is dry, apply many coats of shoe polish. Do not use boot greases on sheaths; they will soften the leather.

Knots and Hitches

Background: A foolproof way to tell an expert camper from a novice is to examine the knots he or she ties. Overhand knots which won't break loose without the aid of a marlin-spike are invariably the work of a beginner. Experts rely on the right knots for the right jobs; they understand that quick-release features (the ability to un-do the knot instantly) is often as important as absolute security. Watch a group of novices dissect the "gobber" knots they've tied in their tent ropes and rain flies and you'll understand why. Nothing is more frustrating than a knot which won't come out!

Outdoors handbooks define dozens of knots and hitches, few of which have much utility. Experts get along very nicely with just three knots and one hitch. These are:

Figure K-3. The double half-hitch.

The double half-hitch

Use this for tying a rope to a tree or any place you want a secure hold that won't slip down.

Figure K-4. The sheet bend.

Sheet bend

Use the sheet bend for tying two ropes together. The knot works wonderfully even when ropes are dissimilar in size. Be sure the free ends of the sheet bend are on the same side as illustrated. The knot will work if the ends are on opposite sides, but it will be less secure.

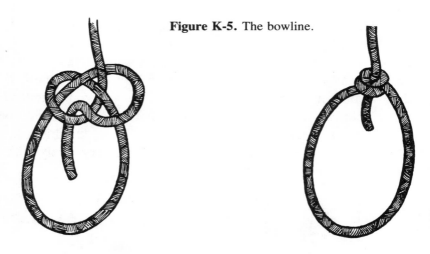

Figure K-5. The bowline.

Bowline

Here's an absolutely secure knot that won't slip. Use it any place you need a non-slip loop at the end of a line. Mountain climbers use this knot for securing their climbing ropes around their waists. If you require absolute security (especially with slippery polypropylene ropes), secure the tail of the finished knot around one arm of the loop with a couple of half hitches.

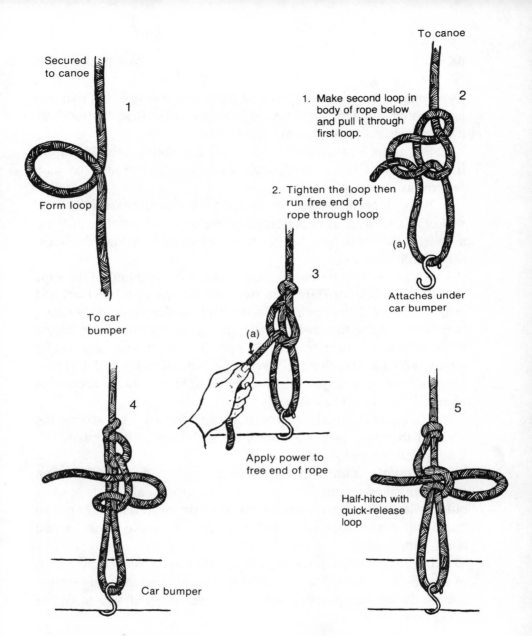

Figure K-6. Power Cinch.

Power-cinch
(also called the "truckers knot")

Use the POWER-CINCH for rigging a clothes line, tying canoes on cars, securing a package on cartop carriers, and anywhere you need a tight lashing that will not slip. The POWER-CINCH has replaced the venerable tautline hitch (see a Boy Scout manual) as *the* hitch for tent guylines. It is faster to rig than the tautline, more versatile, and much more powerful.

Begin the power-cinch by forming a simple overhand loop as in Step 1. Pull the loop through as in step 2, forming the loop *exactly* as shown.

If the loop is formed as in step 2, a simple tug on the rope will eliminate it. This is preferable to the common practice of tying a knot in the loop, which after being exposed to a load is almost impossible to get out.

If you are tying a boat on top of a car, tie one end of the rope to the boat's bow or stern (use two half-hitches or a bowline) and snap the steel S-hook on the other end of the rope to the car's bumper. Run the free end of the rope (a) through the loop in step 2. Now, apply power to the free end. You now have a powerful pulley with a 2:1 mechanical advantage. The POWER-CINCH provides all the power you need to rig a tight line or to secure an object so it positively will not move!

Complete the hitch by securing a double half-hitch around the body of the rope, or use a "quick-release" loop as illustrated.

The quick-release loop

Nothing's more frustrating than untying tight knots when you're breaking camp. The solution is to end all knots with a quick-release loop, which is identical to the procedure you use to transform a would-be overhand knot into a simple "bow" when tying your shoes.

In Figure C-9, a quick-release knot is used to secure the mouth of a nylon stuff sack. Plastic cord-locks (sold in all camping stores) are handy for this purpose but are not necessary if you learn the basic knot.

Lightning

Background: Lightning is a more serious threat than most campers are willing to admit. Next to hypothermia, it is the most dangerous "thing" in the outdoors. Realities of backcountry travel necessarily expose travelers to some risk of being struck by lightning, but this risk may be sharply reduced if you religiously follow these guidelines:

1.   Lightning ordinarily strikes the highest object in its path, so if you pitch your tent in an open field or plateau, be certain there are trees or rock formations of significantly greater height nearby.

2.   A cone of protection extends from the tallest trees or land mass (as the case may be) about 45 degrees outward. Pitch your tent, or walk, canoe, etc., *within* this cone of protection, but stay far enough from its source so that lightning can't jump from the object to you. Lightning may jump a dozen feet or more across water, so don't snug against the shoreline if you're canoeing or boating in an electrical storm. Instead, keep within the cone of protection offered by the shoreline trees.

3.   Lightning may travel along the roots of trees, which may extend dozens of feet outward. If roots are close to the surface of the ground, as in rocky areas where there is little soil cover, sufficient energy may be transmitted along sub-surface roots to pose real danger to anyone standing on the ground above them. Keep this in mind when pitching your tent!

4.   If you're caught outside the cone of protection and suddenly feel electrical energy building (dry hair will stand on end), immediately get as low as possible to reduce the human lightning rod effect.

5.   The notion that non-metal boats are safer than metal ones in a lightning storm has no basis. A lightning strike generates millions of volts, enough to fry anything in its path. Steel ships are occasionally struck by lightning, usually with no ill effects. This suggests that aluminum boats and canoes may in fact be safer than non-metal ones, simply because they more readily dissipate current around the hull into the surrounding water.

If lightning flashes all around, get down low in your boat (below the gunnels) to reduce the lightning rod effect. Again, try to maneuver into the cone of protection offered by the shoreline.

6.   Always check your campsite for tall leaning trees, especially dead ones which may come crashing down on you in a lightning or wind storm.

7.   *If you're in a tent and lightning strikes all around:* Sit up immediately and draw your legs to your chest so that only your buttocks and feet contact the ground. A foam sleeping pad (preferably doubled) placed beneath you may provide enough insulation to keep you from being grounded. If you have no foam rubber sleeping pad, substitute any material which will insulate you from the current.

It is absolutely essential that you maintain the recommended "sitting" position during an electrical storm. In the unlikely event you are struck by lightning while in this position, only your feet and buttocks are apt to burn. But if you're lying flat, electrical energy may pass through your heart and cause death.

Note: Use of a ground cloth *inside* your tent is highly recommended as it ensures you'll have a bone dry tent. All your preventative efforts to outwit lightning will be dashed to the winds if your bedding gets wet. See, TENTS, page 113 for a thorough discussion on the importance of an *interior* ground sheet.

Maps and Map Tricks

Topographic maps in the largest scale you can get, are best for finding your way in the backcountry. The smaller the denominator of the map scale fraction, the larger the scale and more useful the map. The numerator of the fraction indicates map units; the denominator equals ground units. Thus, a scale of 1/24,000 would be interpreted as "one unit of distance on the map equals 24,000 units of distance on the ground. Some representative comparisons are shown below:

1:24,000: One inch on the map equals 2,000 feet on the ground.

1:50,000: One and one-fourth inches equals one mile.

1:62,500: One inch equals approximately one mile.

1:250,000: One inch equals four miles.

For average field use, American maps in 1:62,500 scale, or Canadian maps in 1:50,000 scale are most versatile.

To Order United States Maps
For areas west of the Mississippi River, write to:
>Branch of Distribution
>U.S. Geological Survey
>Federal Center
>Denver, Colorado 80225

For areas east of the Mississippi River, write to:
>Branch of Distribution
>U.S. Geological Survey
>1200 South Eads Street
>Arlington, Virginia 22202

To order Canadian topographic maps, write:
>Canada Map Office
>Department of Energy, Mines and Resources
>625 Booth Street
>Ottawa, Ontario
>Canada K1A OE9

Map Index: Request a free *index to topographic maps* if you do not know precisely what to order. The index will tell you what maps are in print, in what scale, and at what cost. If you roughly define the area of your interest (to the nearest state or Canadian province), you'll receive the appropriate index from the map office.

Colored or monochrome maps? Some 1:50,000 scale Canadian maps may be ordered as monochrome (black and white) editions. Monochrome maps are as accurate and easy to understand as colored versions but are less expensive. They also photocopy perfectly — something to consider if you want to provide low cost maps for a large number of people.

Aerial photos: All maps today are drawn from aerial photos. Photos are available for nearly every inch of land surface and are useful when you need the finest possible detail. Aerial photos are commonly offered as "stereo pairs." With them, you can accurately identify features as small as a boulder or tree. Inexpensive stereoscopes may be purchased from surveying companies and hobby shops.

Order photographs from the same agencies which filled your map orders. There are millions of photos on file, so be sure you accurately indentify the location you need. Best way to get the right pictures is to box in the area of your interest on a large scale topo map. Send this map, with instructions, to the appropriate map office. They'll return your map with the photo order. You can also identify the photo location with precise latitude and longitude coordinates.

Land Use Information Series maps are available for some parts of Canada. They are standard 1:250,000 scale colored maps which have information about wildlife, fishing, geology, ecology, climate, places of interest, etc., over-printed on their surface. *Land Use Information* maps will tell you the precise location of lake trout, the migration route of caribou (and the time of migration), the nesting region for Peregrine falcons, etc. These maps are wonderful for planning trips ... or for dreaming. They cost no more than conventional topographic maps and they're available from the same place. Specify LAND USE INFORMATION SERIES maps when you order. A special index to these maps may obtained free from the Canada Map Office.

Provisional maps (white prints): Most topographic maps are old; some were last field checked decades ago. Topographic features won't change, of course, but manmade ones — roads, trails, buildings, powerlines, etc. — will. If, for example, you're going fishing in Canada, you'll want a map that indicates the location of recently built roads which service the area. Only the most recent topographic maps will indicate the features you want.

However, there may be provisional or white print maps available which have the information you need. Logging and mining companies, and provincial Ministry of Natural Resources, use provisional maps in their daily work. If these current, if unspectacular, maps are available, the MNR or the logging or mining company which services the area will know where to find them. The tourism office in the province of your interest will supply the addresses of MNR area offices. You may also call or write the Canadian Consulate for this information.

Contour lines: The light brown lines overprinted on topographic maps are called contour lines. They indicate the elevation (above sea level) of land features and thus permit you to view the topography in three dimensions rather than two. Entire books have been written about contour lines and their interpretation.However, you'll get along quite nicely if you master these basic rules:

    1.   Contour lines connect points of equal elevation. You will gain (or lose) elevation only when you travel from one contour line to another. If you walk along a contour line, you will "be on the level."

    2.   Closely spaced contour lines indicate lots of elevation change (drop) whereas wide-spaced lines show the opposite (Figures M-1,2).

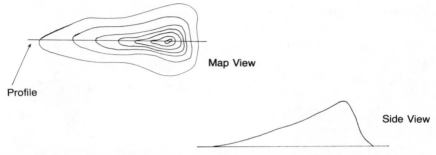

Figure M-1. Basic contour of a long sloping hill indicating the significant drop on the right side of the hill and the gentle slope at left.

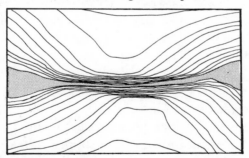

Figure M-2. Contour lines that run very close together and parallel to the banks of a waterway indicate canyons.

    3.   The *contour interval* is the vertical distance between contour lines. Its value in feet or meters is stated in the map margin. If the "CI" is 50 feet, each successive contour line on the map increases or decreases (as the case may be) in elevation by exactly 50 feet.

    4.   The contour interval *is not* the same for all maps, so look closely. Convert meters (all the new Canadian maps are metric) to

feet (one meter equals 3.3 feet) if you're confused by the metric system.

5.   The larger the contour interval, the less clear are the characteristics of the area. In short, a map whose "CI" is 10 feet, gives a clearer picture of the topography than one whose "CI" is 100 feet.

6.   Where contour lines cross or run very close together, you'll find an abrupt drop — a falls or canyon (Figures M-2, M- 3).

7.   The closed or "vee" end of a contour line always points upstream (Figures M-3).

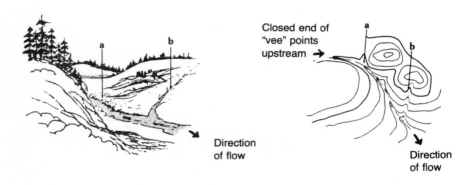

Figure M-3. Stream (b) flows into river (a).

How to waterproof your maps:

1.   Insert them in Zip-lock plastic bags. Giant 12-1/2″ x 16″ Zip-locks are available from most office supply stores.

2.   Cover them with clear contact paper — makes maps waterproof but you can't write on them.

3.   Paint on "Stormproof" — a clear chemical that's especially formulated for use on maps and charts. Order by mail from the Martensen Company, P.O. Box 261, Williamsburg, VA 23185.

4.   Apply "Thompson Water Seal" — an industrial strength chemical that's used for sealing concrete block. "TWS" is available in hardware stores in aerosol cans and tins. Apply it with a foam varnish brush. "TWS" makes maps water-repellent, not waterproof. You can write over it with pen or pencil.

Monofilament Fishing Line

If you're camping out and lose the screw which holds the rim of your glasses to the bow, here's how to fix it. Tie a knot in a piece of monofilament fishing line and thread it through the screw hole. Knot the other end, then use a cigarette lighter to melt both knots to form a tight rivet. The repair will hold for quite some time.

Packs and Packing Methods

Care of packs: Abrasion (dirt!) is the major enemy of the polyurethane coatings used to waterproof packsacks, so wash your packs with a good detergent at least once each camping season. Tree sap (pitch) may be removed with a small amount of cleaning fluid or gasoline. Don't over-do it though; harsh chemicals may dissolve waterproof coatings!

Allow packs to dry thoroughly before you store them away. Wet canvas will mold and damp polyurethane coatings will mildew and peel.

Extending the closing flaps of packsacks: Some packsacks have closing flaps which are too short. The easiest way to extend them without cutting leather or nylon fittings is to sever the flap just behind the closing straps. Sew in a flap extension and re-attach the severed piece.

To improve the abrasion resistance of a soft pack, install a double bottom of the same or heavier fabric. An upholstery shop or shoe repair man can do this for you quickly and inexpensively.

The bottom corners of packs are subject to considerable abrasion. An early (and still excellent) solution was to crown them with glove leather. You can sew small pieces of light-weight leather to abrasion-prone spots or simply paint these areas with epoxy resin. Epoxy will stiffen the fabric and make it virtually tear-proof. Use epoxy to stabilize frayed threads and small holes which are awkward to patch with a sewing machine.

How to pack a soft pack: Now that nearly all packs have internal or external frames, many campers discount the importance of "proper packing." This is unfortunate, for any pack — and your back — will benefit by "doing it right!"

Procedure

1.   Set the pack on its back and first insert along its length, all the soft items that won't gouge your back.

2.   Weight should be kept *as high* as possible. Pack lightweight gear (except crushables) on the bottom, heavyweight items go on top.

3.   For ease of identification and speed of packing, everything should be stored in nylon bags. for example, I commonly keep my extra clothing in a lobster red nylon stuff sack. My lightweight camp mocs go in an orange bag, the stove in a yellow bag, repair kit in a zippered canvas case, raingear in a powder blue sack, etc. The nylon material of "stuff sacks" may be waterproof but the stitching and mouth of the bags are not. So don't depend on waterproof nylon bags to rainproof your outfit. Instead, line your pack (in summer or winter) with a plastic bag and waterproof important items by the double bag sandwich treatment outlined below under *Reliable Waterproofing.*

4.   *Packing the tent:* Most tents have poles which are too long to fit within the confines of a packsack. Consequently, tents and poles should be packed separately, as follows:

a)   Stuff your tent (don't roll it — rolling takes too much time and identically creases the fabric) into its nylon tent bag. Pack poles and stakes into a special heavyduty pole bag with drawstring closure. Sew a loop of nylon webbing to each end of the bag and attach lengths of parachute cord to the loops.

b)   Place your stuffed tent inside your pack and set the pole bag horizontally under the pack flap. Snake the closing straps of the pack through loops in the cord end. Now, your poles can't possibly fall out of your pack!

Reliable waterproofing: Most camping technique books recommend that you waterproof your gear by placing it inside a nylon stuff sack (or pack) that has been lined with one or two plastic garbage bags. If you've ever tried this procedure you know what happens — the thin plastic liner(s) destructs within a few uses. Of course, you can always carry along "a few" extra plastic bags...

Here's a better way — one that won't fail three days into your camping trip:

1.   Stuff your sleeping bag, clothing or other articles into a nylon sack (an abrasion liner) which need not be waterproof.

2.   Place this sack *inside* an absolutely watertight plastic bag. Twist, fold over and secure the mouth of the plastic bag with a loop of shock-cord.

3.   Set this unit *inside* a second nylon bag, which need not be watertight. Your articles are now completely protected against rain and a canoe capsize. Note that the delicate plastic liner is sandwiched between two layers of tough nylon, out-of-contact with abrasive materials. Use this "sandwich bag" method to pack everything you must keep dry. This is the best way to protect a sleeping bag that rides obtrusively on the outside frame of a backpack.

Hip belt and tumpline: Most backpackers know the advantages of a hip belt, but few appreciate the worth of a tumpline. A tumpline consists of a wide leather or fabric strap which is secured to the "ears" (sides of the pack at shoulder level) of a packsack. The packer places this strap just above his forehead, grabs the tumpline near his head, leans forward, and trucks confidently down the trail. The early voyageurs carried hundreds of pounds of furs by this method, and packers in undeveloped countries still rely on the system.

Tumplines are most useful when ascending steep hills, as they take considerable weight off the packstraps. To make a tumpstrap for your pack, simply sew a D-ring to each side of your pack at shoulder   height,   and   mount   the   tumpline   across   them.

Pack pockets: Sew up some small envelope-style pockets and attach them to the outside of your pack with heavyduty glove snaps or Velcro strips. These "pack pockets" will add versatility to your hiking outfit. If you attach mating strips of Velcro to the inner walls of your tent, sidewalls or thwarts of your canoe or boat, etc., your pack pockets can be quickly re-mounted to provide added convenience.

Quin-Zee Hut

Background: A quin-zee is the white man's version of the traditional Eskimo igloo. It's made by piling up snow then digging out the center, rather than by carefully laying snow blocks. Quin-zees are as warm, as strong, and as spacious as igloos but they take much longer to build. Compared to igloos, they are terribly ugly. An Eskimo snow house is a work of art; a quin-zee retains the appearance of a shlocked-together snow pile (which is exactly what it is). Nonetheless, quin-zees are practical for base camp travel in winter and as emergency survival dwellings. Kids build them just for fun and occasionally someone makes news by carving a garage-size quin-zee from a giant snowbank. Quin-zees are similar to snow caves, which are also built from packed snow. Snow caves, however, are hollowed out from an existing packed drift, which is faster and simpler than piling snow. Both structures serve the same function — that of keeping you warm and dry regardless of the weather outside.

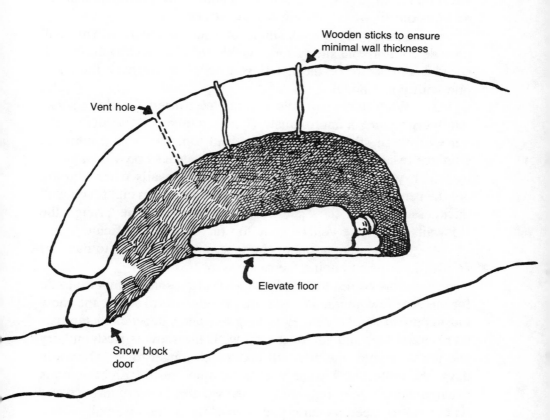

Wooden sticks to ensure
minimal wall thickness

Vent hole

Elevate floor

Snow block
door

Figure Q-1. Quin-zee hut.

You don't need a thick layer of snow to build a quin-zee. You can simply haul in what you need or scrape a thin surface layer of snow to provide sufficient building material.

Building the quin-zee

1. First decide on the size. A 10-12 foot diameter is about right for two people. Most snow campers make their huts too small, so err on the large side. You can easily adjust the interior dimensions to a custom fit when you dig out the structure.

2. Pile up snow to a height of about seven feet. This will provide comfortable sitting room inside for both occupants. You'll speed manufacture of the hut if you occasionally pack the snow pile with your shovel.

3. When the snow pile is complete, insert foot long sticks into the structure at approximate 18 inch intervals. "Porcupine" the hut with these sticks all around and on top. Don't stop until the quin-zee resembles a medieval mace. These sticks provide a gauge by which you can judge the thickness of the walls when you dig out the center. It is essential to maintain a minimum eight inch wall thickness. Without the "gauge," you'll shovel right through the sidewalls, and once you've gone too far, repair is difficult.

4. If you want a tunnel entrance, now's the time to build it. Don't forget to porcupine the tunnel.

5. Now comes the hard part — finding something else to do for the next few hours. The structure needs time to settle, the snow must contract and harden. How long this takes depends on temperature, humidity, and age of the snow. If the snow is fresh and dry and it's very cold, the pile will take much longer to set. On warm days, the molecular change will occur much faster. Eight hours is usually enough time, regardless of the weather. *Do not* throw water on the hut to speed its cure; you'll wind up with an ice ball — one you can't dig out or breathe inside of!

6. When the structure has hardened, prepare to dig. You'll need a small shovel and a friend. You'll get very wet from falling snow so wear rain gear or highly water repellent clothing. Dig out the tunnel entrance through to the center, passing carved snow to your partner outside. Now, it's simply a matter of sculpting the interior to suit your fancy. Just remember to stop digging when you see the porcupine "hairs." You need to maintain an eight inch

minimum wall thickness! Do not remove the porcupine sticks from the structure; doing so will weaken the hut.

7. *Finishing the interior:* As everyone knows, warm air rises while cold air does the opposite. For this reason, you need to elevate the sleeping area a foot or so for additional warmth. While you're doing this you can also carve some "pockets" into the sidewalls, in which to place small items. Make a small shelf for your candle — a single candle will light the entire structure and raise its temperature considerably.

8. *Vent hole:* It's not absolutely essential to cut a vent hole in the roof, but it will make for a better exchange of air if you do. Simply punch a ski pole through the roof or pull out one of the porcupine sticks. Don't panic if the hole eventually fills with snow and closes. You'll get plenty of fresh air through the doorway, and the quin-zee walls are porous.

9. *Doorway:* If you have a tunnel entrance to break the wind, you don't need a door. However, a snow block, angled across the entry way will reduce heat loss without significantly affecting ventilation. Just be sure you don't close the snow block door completely.

Tip: A length of nylon parachute cord makes an acceptable snow knife for cutting blocks. Just saw the cord back and forth through the snow until the block is free. This procedure will only work with "old snow," whose molecular structure has compacted.

Warning: The heat generated by two or three bodies in a small quin-zee will easily maintain an interior hut temperature of 20 or more degrees Fahrenheit. In fact, temperature may rise above freezing if you're not careful. The danger is not in being too cold; it is allowing the structure to overheat. If the temperature goes above freezing, the interior walls will melt and ice up, ventilation will cease, the structure will drip water and you'll have an intolerable mess. So watch your thermometer — and your hut temperature — carefully.

Sleeping inside the quin-zee: As stated, interior temperatures are apt to maintain a balmy 20 degrees Fahrenheit, even in sub-zero weather, so you don't need an arctic sleeping bag for comfort. Any three season bag will do, providing you have plenty of insulation beneath you. You're sleeping on ice, remember?

Your first sleeping layer is a waterproof plastic ground sheet.

Atop this place foam pads, carpeting, cardboard — anything that will insulate your body from the cold ground. If you have an open-cell foam trail pad, a two inch thickness (or greater) will be required for comfort. A five-eighths inch thick closed-cell foam pad may provide enough warmth. You need *much more* insulation below than on top!

Common fears: There are two... 1) "I'll die from carbon-monoxide poisoning." 2) "The hut will collapse and smother me." Both concerns are unfounded. You'll get plenty of air through the entry way and vent hole, even in the unlikely event the quin-zee freezes over. As to strength, there is no contest. Snow huts gain strength as they age. I doubt a polar bear could crush a week old quin-zee!

Tip: If you plan to use the shelter for several nights, chip away the ice build-up on the inner walls each day. This will maintain "breathability" of the structure.

Important tip: The entry way of a quin-zee or snow cave should always be placed on the *windward* side of the structure. If wind-driven snow begins while you sleep, sufficient snow could pile up on the leeward side of the hut to seal a leeward entrance. This could be quite serious (deadly!) in a snow cave, especially in a blizzard. It's always wise to keep a small shovel in a snow hut, just in case you need to dig out in the morning!

Rainfly (Tarp)

Background: This is your most useful item in a rainy day camp. Under it you'll comfortably prepare meals, make repairs, and otherwise enjoy a day that might be soured by rain. The value of a fly is obvious, whether you're camped on a remote mountain vista or in the gentle confines of a state park. It requires skill and a bit of weather knowledge to pitch a drum-tight fly in a howling storm, yet anyone can learn how in less than an hour. A well-rigged rainfly truly exemplifies the experts' edge.

Materials: A 10 foot by 10 foot (or larger) nylon tarp for every four people. I ordinarily rig a single fly in modified lean-to configuration, but for severe storms, I mate the pair into a giant open tent that everyone can crowd under.

Customize your fly according to the directions in Figure R-1. Install *five* grommets or nylon web loops (loops are more secure than grommets) per side (most flies come with only three) and five loops on the fly face. Be sure to reinforce all loops with heavy material. A ripstop nylon backing is not strong enough.

87

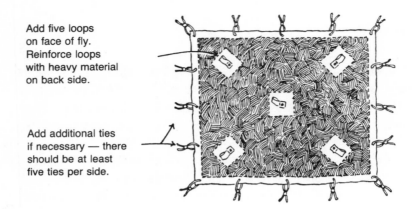

Add five loops on face of fly. Reinforce loops with heavy material on back side.

Add additional ties if necessary — there should be at least five ties per side.

Figure R-1. Customizing the Rain Tarp: Add ties to all grommets and sew five equally spaced loops to the face.

Attach foot long loops of parachute cord to all perimeter loops and knot the cords so they'll stay put. Permanently install a 25 foot length of line on the center face loop.

Cut a half dozen 15 foot lengths of chute cord and coil and tie them. Store these, the fly, and six lightweight aluminum tent stakes in a nylon bag so everything will be handy when you need it.

Pitching the fly: There are so many ways to pitch a fly that it's probably pointless to recommend a single method. Nonetheless, here's an absolutely wind-stable design that can be erected single-handed in three minutes flat.

Procedure

1. Locate two trees at least 12 feet apart and string a drum-tight line between them about 6 feet off the ground. Use 2 half-hitches at one end of the rope and a power-cinch with a quick-release knot at the other end (see page 65 for a review of knots).

2. Take the pair of ties at one corner of your fly and wind one tie of the set around the rope in a clockwise direction and the other tie in a counterclockwise direction. Take at least 4 turns around the rope. Secure the ties with a simple overhand bow.

3. Pull the other corner of the open end of the fly tight along the rope and secure it with the ties, as in number 2 above. The tie wrappings will provide sufficient tension to keep the corners of the tarp from slipping inward along the rope when the fly is buffeted by wind.

4. Secure all remaining ties to the rope with an overhand bow. (By securing the fly at several points along the length of its open end, rather than just at the corners, as is commonly done, you distribute the strain across a wide area, thus increasing the strength of the fly.)

5. Go to the back of the fly, pull it out tight, and stake.

6. Run the center cord over a tree limb or a rope strung just above and behind the fly. Snug up the center cord (use a power-cinch with a quick-release) to pull the center of the fly out. Add additional lines on the face, as necessary to prevent pooling of rain water.

7. Secure the sides of the fly with extra cord, and complete all knots with a quick-release loop. Use a quick-release sheetbend to attach extension lines to the fly.

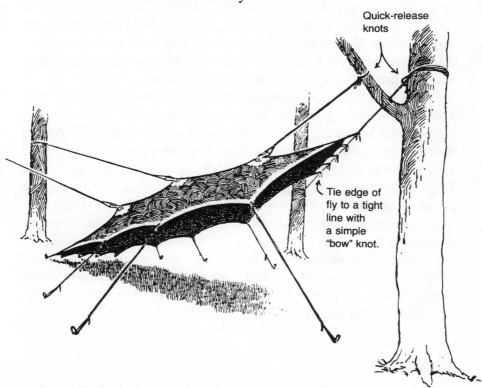

Figure R-2. A customized rain tarp can be rigged in less than three minutes and will withstand 30 mile per hour winds.

If you build a fire under the fly: Smoke will accumulate in the void produced by the fly face unless you provide adequate ventilation at ground level. This means unstaking the back and raising the fly a foot or more to provide a breezeway at this point.

To rig twin flies: Rig your second fly opposite the first, in an identical manner. However, you'll need to overlap a foot or so of material (back to the second grommet) over the ridge line so rain won't filter between the two tarps.

Secure one tie on each side of the fly to the ridge line and let the remaining perimeter ties hang loose. In wind-blown rain you may need to weight these free ties with a heavy stick or extend them to a secure spot with lengths of parachute cord. How best to do this will become obvious once you have the basic structure in place.

If weight is critical and you have no rain tarp

If restrictions on weight or bulk preclude carrying a nylon rain tarp, modify the corners of your tent floor so that they can be released from the fly (or ground, as the case may be) and pushed aside to provide a dry place to cook and work.

For example, to rig a standard Eureka Timberline tent by this method, remove (you may have to cut them off!) the four steel rings at the tent floor corners which contain the pole pins. Attach a heavy brass snap hook to each of these rings, then re-install the pole pins and re-close the rings (it may be easier to replace the cut rings with steel split rings). Now, attach the brass snaps to the nylon webbing at the floor corners. This will enable you to disconnect the ring/pin system from the tent floor corners *without* dropping the staked fly.

Now, push aside the tent body (you need only disconnect two of the four adjacent floor corners) and climb under the exoskeleton-supported fly. Any tent which has a separate rainfly can be easily modified by this procedure.

Rain Gear

Background: Rain gear has become quite stylish. Some parkas now feature hoods with integral bills that turn with your head, under-arm zippers for better ventilation, drip-proof pockets, waist and hem cords, and much more. These niceties are nice, of course, but they won't keep you dry. What will, is a sensibly designed garment that is constructed of genuinely waterproof material.

Fabrics: There are those that work and those that don't. Some work "sometimes." And the difference between them is not necessarily a function of price. In fact, some of the best (most watertight, that is) rain wear costs less than some of the worst!

If you want reliable raingear at a reasonable price, see what the professionals are wearing. Foresters, wildlife management people and construction workers all require tough garments that are absolutely waterproof. Rain garments like these are available at every industrial supply store. The new industrial rain suits are constructed of fabrics which are similar, and often identical to, those used on the best foul weather sailing suits. But because there are no pockets, no under-arm zippers, and often no hoods to boost the price, they cost much less.

Camping stores also feature a wealth of different rain gear. Invariably, el-cheapo models are the best buy, that is, if you're willing to seal the seams yourself with the special glue provided.

At the other extreme are PVC, neoprene, and hypalon-coated garments that will keep you dry no matter how long or hard it rains. And these suits are worth their high cost if you absolutely must stay dry in foul weather.

Gore-Tex: Gore-Tex rain wear continues to be popular despite its very high price, somewhat crinkly hand, and its occasional unreliability. The product seems to work well when new, but in time, it often leaks, subtly at first, then without embarrassment. Failure seems somehow related to "degree of use."

Gore-Tex is wonderful for winter skiing and those transition periods between rain and snow. And it makes a fine paddling shirt for whitewater kayaking. Though Gore-Tex has been steadily improved since its inception a decade ago, many experts still don't trust it for use over extended periods of heavy rain.

Style: Whether you hike, canoe, motorcycle, backpack or sail, you'll be happiest with a generously sized two-piece rainsuit. Ponchos provide inadequate protection and may be dangerous in a boat upset. Below-the-knee rainshirts are ideal for casual fishing and auto camping but are otherwise impractical.

You'll put on and remove raingear frequently between showers so select garments which are easy to slip on and off. Select jackets with zippered or snap fronts rather than anorak models which fit over the head. Pants which have an elastic or corded waist band are much more versatile than those with bibs.

Tip: Tear out the elastic waist band of rain pants and substitute a fabric cord and cordlock. Elastic loses its stretch in time and rain pants will fall down. A cord provides quick, positive adjustments.

Avoid pants with snaps or Velcro tabs at the bottom. These restrict ventilation. Besides, primitive man learned long ago that water doesn't flow uphill! Ankle closures are only useful for mountaineering above the timberline.

Pant legs should be cut oversize so you can easily slip them on over heavy trousers or boots. Some expensive rain pants feature baffled zippers at the ankles. Straight cut pant legs go over boots just as easily and are less costly to manufacture. Zippers eventually gum up with debris and fail —they're just another gimmick to drive up costs.

Tip: If you want to learn all there is to know about *good* rain gear, check out the best foul weather sailing suits. The only frills you'll see on these garments are ones that work. Now, compare your observations to rain garments in camping shops!

Jacket fit: Buy your rain parka a full size larger than you think you need, large enough so you can wear several layers of clothes beneath. Rain gear that looks trim in the store will be hot and restrictive in the field.

Color: Color is a personal choice, though navy blue garments outsell all others by a wide margin. And that's unfortunate, for this color *attracts* mosquitoes which invariably come out in between showers!

Hoods: A traditionally styled souwester hat is much more functional than a restrictive hood. However, if you select a hooded parka, be sure the zipper comes right to your nose. Those which stop at the chin must have a throat strap to seal off the neck area or they'll admit cold air and rain.

Pockets, seams, and zippers: Two *covered* pockets are more than enough in any rain jacket. Additional pockets add weight, bulk, and cost and threaten the integrity of the waterproof construction. The fewer the seams in any rain garment, the more watertight it will be. Except to close the front of a jacket, the value of zippers is over-rated. Under-arm zippers (which are added for ventilation) keep out rain only if you don't raise your arms. And zippered flies in rain pants usually leak within a few seconds of instantly.

Waterproofing standards: The U.S. army requires a garment to withstand a minimum of 25 pounds per square inch (PSI) water pressure in order to earn the title of "waterproof." At first thought, this industry-accepted minimum seems adequate, that is until you realize a person may exert that much pressure (or more!) simply by sitting on the edge of a boat seat. Kneel down or plant your elbows firmly in the duff and you may experience similar results. In all likelihood, minimally rated rain wear will not keep you dry!

Good rain clothes will withstand two or three times the amount of water pressure specified by the military, but even this may not be enough for strenuous field use. Then, there's the matter of abrasion. Every time you put on or take off your rain parka, or move while wearing it, a micro-thin layer of waterproof chemical is scraped off the fabric. In time, leaks develop.

One answer to the abrasion problem is to sew a liner into the garment. But liners add weight, cost, and bulk. They also absorb sweat and are slow to dry. A better solution is to *insist* on a fabric with a minimum 100 PSI waterproof coating. And for really severe applications (like foul-weather sailing), you may want to consider the merits of a fabric which boasts a 150 PSI (or greater) rating.

Unfortunately, manufacturers of rain wear do not usually advertise the PSI ratings of their products. For comparison: A Kenyon Industries light polyurethane coating ("Light K-Kote," as specified on the garment label) will average 25 to 50 PSI on the Mullen hydrostatic test, which is used to determine waterproofness of fabrics. But a "Super (double) K-Kote" treatment will run 100 PSI or more, which makes it suitable for all but the meanest applications.

Tip: You'll increase the effectiveness of your rain gear if you double the thickness of abrasion prone areas — knees, elbows, and *especially* the seat. All you need is a sewing machine and some matching fabric. And don't forget to seal the seams you've sewn!

Rain gear for children: (See Children, Tips for camping with, page 23).

When not to wear rain gear: Some authorities suggest you eliminate a windbreaker from your clothing list and instead rely on your rain parka for wind protection. Frankly, I think this is bad advice. Every time you lean against a tree or scrape a rock, abrasion takes its toll. In no time leaks develop. If you want your rain gear to last more than a season or two, use it only for its intended purpose and switch to a windshell when the need arises.

Tip: If you wear your rain coat over your nylon wind-shell, you'll reduce abrasion to the waterproof inner coating (the shell acts as a liner). Twin jackets will also keep you warmer and drier than a single waterproof garment.

What to wear under rain gear: Don't wear cotton! It absorbs perspiration and super-cools the body. Since perspiration cannot escape through a waterproof covering, a wet, clammy feeling is guaranteed!

If you wear a pure wool or polyester pile shirt over a polypropylene undershirt, you'll stay dry and in command no matter how hard it rains. Moisture will pass harmlessly through the polypropylene weave into the wool or pile where it will be absorbed and wicked from fiber to fiber. It will take many hours to sufficiently load a wool or pile garment with enough moisture to cause concern. And if your rain clothes are at all ventilated (they should be), enough water vapor will be spilled to the environment to ensure your comfort no matter how hot or cold the rain.

Tip: Store rain clothes in a nylon stuff sack between uses. This will keep them clean and eliminate the abrasion which results from stuffing clothing into packs.

Care and repair of rain gear: Hand wash in detergent. Air dry thoroughly before storing. Store rain gear on hangers so air will circulate. Don't keep these items in confining stuff sacks — polyurethane coatings *will* mildew!

Patch holes and tears with matching material. Any portable sewing machine will work. Easiest way to get "matching fabric" is to cut up the stuff sack which came with the garment. Seal all stitching with "seam sealer," which you can buy at all camping shops.

Ropes

Background: To most campers, a rope is a rope, and they make no distinction between manila, polypropylene, dacron, and nylon. That's too bad, because certain rope materials and weaves excel in different applications. What works best as water ski tow line is completely inappropriate for rigging a rainfly. Here are some differences and points to consider when choosing ropes:

1. *Flexibility:* Flexible ropes accept knots more willingly than stiffer weaves but are more likely to snag in their own coils. Choose flexible ropes for tying canoes on cars and any place a proper lashing is essential. Stiff ropes are best for throwing lines (life-saving), boat mooring and tracking lines, and general use around water.

2. *Slipperiness:* A slippery rope is always a nuisance. Some ropes, notably those made from polypropylene, are so slippery that they will not retain knots.

3. *Diameter versus strength:* Modern synthetic lines are very strong. Even one-eighth inch diameter parachute cord has more breaking strength than you will probably ever need. However, large diameter ropes are much easier to handle, and less likely to snag, than small diameter ones. Quarter-inch diameter rope is about minimal for heavyduty camping applications. Eighth inch diameter parachute cord is the recommended camp utility cord.

Note: There are several grades of parachute cord. Avoid the cheap stuff that's commonly sold at hardware stores.

Types of rope

Nylon is the most popular fiber for utility rope, and for good reason. It's strong, light, immune to rot, and inexpensive. On the negative side, it stretches *considerably* when wet, shrinks when dry. This makes it a bad choice for mooring boats, for canoe tracking lines, and anywhere you need a rope that won't change dimensions. Nylon also degrades in the sun. A nylon rope may lose half or more of its strength in a single season if it's continually exposed to the weather.

The two most common weaves are the "three-strand-braided," and "sheathed-core." Braided rope is very soft and flexible but it cannot be "flame-whipped" after it's cut. The ends of nylon and polypropylene ropes are usually sealed after cutting by melting them in the flame of a cigarette lighter. Three-strand-braided rope simply unravels when heat is applied. It must be whipped the traditional Navy way by winding the ends with waxed string, or by dipping them in plastic whipping compound (available at marinas).

Sheathed nylon ropes (there are many variations) feature a central core surrounded by a woven nylon sheath. This construction is slightly less flexible than the braided type but is pliant enough for camp use. Sheathed ropes flame-whip easily and do not unravel. Quarter-inch diameter stock is ideal for rigging clothes lines, tying gear on cars and trailers, and other utility applications.

Polypropylene: The choice lies between round, three-strand stiff-braided line and the cheap flat-woven stuff sold in hardware stores. It's no contest; the stiffer line excels in every category.

Polypropylene has two advantages over nylon: It does not degrade in sunlight, and it doesn't stretch when wet. These characteristics make it ideal for use around water.

Ropes for mountaineering: Some types of mountaineering rope make excellent utility line. The choice lies between "three-strand-hard lay" construction, or the kermantle type (a core of braided or twisted strands — the kern, is covered by a protective braided sheath — the mantle). Three-strand rope is much cheaper than kermantle and it has a stiffer hand, which makes it ideal for lining canoes, mooring boats, and anywhere you need a snag-free rope that won't fail. Recreational Equipment, Inc. (REI, P.O. Box C-88125, Seattle, WA 98188) sells a hard-braided rope called *Skyline II*, which in quarter-inch diameter (3/8 and 7/16 inch diameter is also available), makes excellent multi-purpose line. Quarter-inch diameter *Skyline II* is rated to break at 1,670 pounds, which means it's much stronger than comparable hardware store rope. *Skyline II* is sold by the foot and is priced below most equivalent sized nylon utility ropes.

Dacron line is *the* material for sailboat sheet and mooring lines. It's wonderfully strong, beautifully soft, and frightfully expensive. If you're a sailor you know all about dacron line. Advantages of dacron over nylon include: 1) Very little wet-stretch/dry shrinkage; 2) It is immune to the degrading effects of sunlight — a feature which is very important on boats which are exposed to the weather.

Manila and hemp have almost gone the way of the passenger pigeon. These natural fiber ropes (Manila is far superior to hemp!) have a nice hand; they coil beautifully, offer a textured grip, and they even smell nice, but they rot easily, and for their weight, aren't very strong. I can think of no reason to use natural fiber ropes when better synthetics are available for about the same price.

Tip: Abrasion is the major enemy of rope, so occasionally wash your ropes with detergent to remove ground-in grime. You'll prolong the life of your ropes considerably.

Rope Tricks

Nylon utility ropes are best coiled and bound by the old Navy method indicated below:

Steps

1.   Coil the rope and put your thumb through the coils to hold them in place. Leave about three feet of rope uncoiled (Figure R-3).

2.   Grasp the rope in one hand and pinch it at the waist to form an "eye." Coil the free end (tail) around the rope, upwards towards the eye. Overlap the first coil to lock it in place. Wind evenly and tightly (Figure R-4).

Figure R-3.   **Figure R-4.**

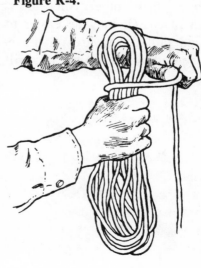

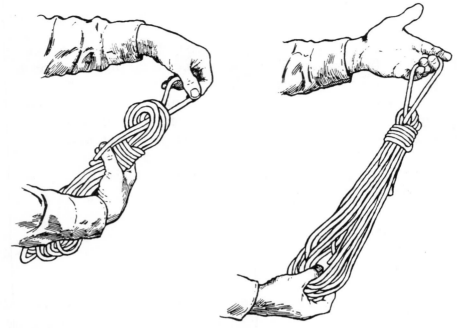

Figure R-5.   **Figure R-6.**

    3.   Form a loop near the end of the tail and pass it through the eye (Figure R-5).

    4.   Grasp the collar (wound coils) in one hand and the rope body in the other. Slide the collar up to the rope to lock the loop in place. (It may be easier to hold the collar firmly in one hand and pull downward on the body of the rope.) The rope is now secured; a pull on the tail will release it (Figure R-6).

Saw (Folding)

A folding saw is one of your most useful camp tools. On a rainy day you may be unable to get a fire going without one! Aluminum-framed saws are flimsy and their triangular shapes don't permit you to cut big logs. Best camp saw I've seen is a full-stroke rectangular model called the FAST BUCKSAW. It's constructed of hard maple and has an easily replaceable 21-inch blade (refills are available from the manufacturer or at any hardware store). When assembled, it's so rigid you'd swear it was a one-piece model. These saws are available by mail from FAST BUCKSAW, INC., 110 East Fifth St., Hastings, MN 55033.

Tips: Keep your disassembled folding saw in a nylon bag with drawstring closure. This will keep the parts cleaner and speed assembly time.

Occasionally wipe tree sap from saw blades with a rag dipped in gasoline or alcohol. This will improve cutting performance and slow rusting of the blade.

Shovel

A three-quarter inch diameter, foot long aluminum tube, flattened at one end, makes an ideal camp shovel. Use it for burying fire remains, fish viscera, and human wastes where proper disposal facilities do not exist. (See Ethics section, page 42, for the proper way to dispose of wastes in the backcountry.)

Shower

You can make an effective portable shower by attaching a light plastic hose and shower head to a folding plastic water jug. Use a long hose and drive the system with foot pressure. If stove fuel or wood (to heat water) is in short supply, consider bringing along a commercial "Sun Shower," which is similar to the above system except for its special heat absorbing fabric. Sun showers can be purchased at most camp shops and marinas. They are quite popular with yachtsmen.

Skis (cross-country)

Under certain conditions, the surface of cross-country skis will load up with crusty snow and impede performance. To prevent this ice build-up, occasionally apply a coat of paste wax to the top of your skis.

The wire bailer on cross-country ski bindings can "flip out" of the binding and be lost in a bad fall. A short length of parachute cord which connects the bailer and binding (holes are drilled in most bindings for this purpose) will keep these parts together.

You'll add *considerable* strength to bamboo ski poles if you wrap nylon strapping tape around them at approximate two-inch intervals.

Sleeping Bags

Background: This is your most important item. With care, a good sleeping bag will last half a life-time, even with almost regular use. Though tremendous advancements in insulation technology are in the wind, at this writing there are only three types of sleeping bag fill which are worth considering for serious use in the backcountry. These are goose down, Cellanse "Polarguard," and Dupont "Quallofil." Any of these products will serve you well if they're sewn into a well constructed bag.

Principles of sleeping bag design

    1.   The smaller the bag, the less area it will have to insulate. Translation: Confining mummy bags are much warmer for their weight than roomy rectangular ones.

    2.   Most heat loss from a sleeping bag occurs through the open head end. It's nearly impossible to seal the open end of a rectangular style sleeping bag so that warm air won't escape. (One solution is to install a collar — see Figure C-6 for details.) For this reason integral hoods are mandatory on sleeping bags that will be used for cold weather camping.

    Tip: An effective makeshift collar can be made from a sweater or scarf. Drape the garment across your chest and bunch the fabric around your neck and shoulders, feathering it to the adjacent sleeping bag fabric. This will eliminate drafts and increase warmth.

    3.   Inexpensive mummy style sleeping bags, and all rectangular models, are built with a "flat" foot, which means the material is simply folded in half at the foot end, and a zipper is installed around the edge (as in a typical station-wagon sleeping bag). A "boxed" foot design, though more costly to manufacture, is much more comfortable. Here, a foot high circular panel is sewn in at the bottom (like the end of a tin can) which allows you to maintain a comfortable "toes up" position without bearing against tight material.

    4.   A full length zipper which runs from foot to chin is a must. Bags with half-length zippers become impossibly hot in warm weather.

Categories

    Down and synthetic sleeping bags are generally categorized as:

    a)   *Summer weight* — comfortable in temperatures to freezing.

    b)   *Three-season* — warm to about 10-15 degrees Fahrenheit.

c)   *Winter* — good to 20 below zero or more. There are some special arctic bags which go much lower than that.

Note: "Comfort ratings" are speculative. Few sleeping bags are as warm as their manufacturers suggest!

Which sleeping bag for you?

Most people select three-season models thinking they represent the greatest value for the money. Wrong! The typical three season sleeping bag becomes *too warm* when temperatures rise above 50 degrees Fahrenheit, which means they are next to worthless for average summer use.

Only if you do considerable primitive camping in the spring and fall, should you buy a three-season bag. Otherwise, a lighter, less costly summer bag will be a better buy. Tent temperatures commonly run about 10 degrees warmer than the outside environment, so a good summer bag will keep you toasty well below freezing. In really cold weather, you can mate your summer bag with an outer or inner liner, or a blanket.

Which is best, down or synthetics? Down bags are lighter, warmer, more compact, and have a more "gentle hand" than any of the synthetics. If you've ever slept under a down comforter, you know what I mean. Good down is also much more resilient and long lived than synthetics. For an equivalent weight of fill, down has a lower and wider temperature comfort range. This means down will keep you warmer when it's cold, and cooler when it's warm, than will a synthetic.

For example: Consider two three-season sleeping bags, one down, one Polarguard or Quallofil. Both bags are rated to 10 degrees Fahrenheit. Finished weight of the down bag will be *at least* a pound less than either synthetic and it will compact into a much smaller space. The synthetic bag will become too warm when the temperature reaches 50 degrees Fahrenheit, while the down bag will remain quite comfortable, even at 60 degrees.

However, good down sleeping bags are much more expensive than equivalently rated synthetic ones, and you can't beat them around as much. And wet down is almost impossible to dry under typical field conditions. Because down is a natural fiber, it absorbs body moisture, which in damp winter conditions can be serious. For this reason, experienced winter hikers usually select Polarguard or Quallofil sleeping bags.

Question: If down dries so slowly, shouldn't we eliminate it from consideration for summer use too? Absolutely not! If you "sandwich pack" your sleeping bag as I recommend in the packing section (page 80) and storm-proof your tent accordingly (see page 117), you will *never* get your bedding wet. I guarantee it! Only unskilled idiots get sleeping bags — or anything else — wet on camping trips. I've made some pretty substantial wilderness trips over the past 30 years and I've always managed to keep my down bag dry. If you follow the tips I've outlined, you will too.

Buy what you can afford; but whatever you buy, make sure it has a hood to keep your head warm, a full-length two-way zipper to keep your feet cool, and a temperature range which matches the environment in which you'll camp. If you choose a "mummy bag" — and most experienced campers do — try it in the store before you buy it. Mummy bags come in different lengths and girths; some are quite restrictive while others are surprisingly roomy. If a bag feels tight in the store, you won't like it in the field.

Winter sleeping bags are more generously sized than summer ones to allow dressing space inside. Winter campers usually take their clothing and canteens to bed so they need space for all these "rummage sale" items. The typical polyester-filled winter bag weighs five pounds or more. Summer weight bags may weigh half that.

Packing the sleeping bag: Sleeping bags (discounting station-wagon types) should be *stuffed* not rolled. Zippers should be closed to prevent galling of the material. Just grab the foot end of the bag and stuff it, handful by handful into its nylon sack. This is easier on the fabric and fill than traditional rolling.

Do not store sleeping bags in stuff sacks; you'll wear out the filler in no time. Instead, keep sleeping bags in a breathable cotton sack (a pillow case works fine), or store them flat or on hangers.

Cleaning your sleeping bag

Down bags and other down garments: Hand-washing is the best way to clean any down-filled item. Nonetheless, manufacturers usually recommend "dry cleaning" on down product labels simply because so many down items have been ruined by improper machine washing. Make no mistake: Dry cleaning with powerful perchlorethylene solvents will reduce the loft and warmth of a down bag. But it will not destroy it. Improper washing will! Here's the recommended procedure for *handwashing:*

Directions

1.   You'll need a huge basin to wash your sleeping bag. A bathtub is ideal.

2.   Use luke-warm water and any mild soap. I've had good luck with "Woolite," "Ivory Snow," "Ivory liquid," "Basic-H" and other liquid dishwashing detergents. There are also some special down soaps which may or may not be worth their high price.

3.   Place the sleeping bag into the soap solution and sponge the shell thoroughly. Rub gently at stubborn spots. *Do not* use "Spray and Wash" or stain removers! The shells of sleeping bags are very tightly woven to contain the down, so it may require many hours for wash water to work through them.

Allow the bag to soak in the wash water for an hour or so, then squish the bag gently with wide-spread hands. Carefully, work wash water well into the down. A couple hours of additional soaking and frequent "squishing" should remove most of the dirt.

4.   *Rinsing the bag:* Drain the tub and gently press soapy water out of the article with both hands, fingers spread wide apart. Don't lift or wring out the article. A water-filled sleeping bag is very heavy and the delicate baffles may tear if you rough-house the project.

A minimum of *two* rinse cycles is recommended. You absolutely must get all the soap out or the down will mat when it dries.

5.   Gently place the thoroughly rinsed sleeping bag into a large plastic clothes basket for ease-of-handling. Now, it's off to your laundromat with several dollars change in hand.

6.   Place the incompletely rinsed bag into an "extractor" (a high speed centrifuge) and spin out the remaining water. If your laundromat does not have one of these machines, a large washing machine, set on spin dry will work. One pass through the extractor or two passes through the washing machine will safely exhaust nearly all the water.

7.   Next, place the bag in a large commercial clothes dryer set on very low heat. Be sure the dryer puts out *low* heat! If it does not, run it with the door ajar (jam a magazine through the door

hinge over the safety button so the machine will continue to run) to bleed heat. Check the progress of the bag every 10 minutes.

Some people place a terry cloth towel into the dryer to absorb the static electricity. This seems to speed drying.

It will take you a full day to wash your sleeping bag!

Warning: Do not attempt to dry a sleeping bag in family sized clothes dryers. The heat is concentrated over too small an area. You may, however, safely spin-dry your sleeping bag in your home washing machine if a commercial extractor is not available.

When to clean your sleeping bag

Once every year or two is often enough, even if you use your bag a lot. A down bag will lose some loft and resiliency with the first washing. Additional washings seem to have no adverse effect.

Some campers never wash their sleeping bags; they believe that washing will ruin them. But body oils and dirt *will* accumulate and the insulative value of the bag will decrease accordingly. It's a catch 22. My advice? Keep your bag as clean as possible and wash it carefully when the occasion demands.

How to wash Polarguard and Quallofil sleeping bags

Polyester-filled sleeping bags and garments cannot be dry-cleaned. The cleaning fluid will destroy the fill. These garments are best handwashed in the same manner as down bags. Yes, you can machine wash them successfully. However, most sleeping bags are too large to be safely washed in family sized washing machines — some abrasion, stretching of stitches, etc., is sure to result. If you must machine wash your bag, use one of the large front loading commercial machines. Even then, my vote goes to hand washing.

Polyester-filled jackets, vests and other small items may be safely washed in most home machines (gentle cycle only). But, they must be dried with low (under 120° Fahrenheit) heat — or better, no heat!

Do's and don'ts for sleeping bags

Don't roll sleeping bags; stuff them!

Don't yank sleeping bags out of stuff sacks; pull gently.

Don't leave sleeping bags stuffed for long periods of time.

Don't machine wash down sleeping bags.

Don't dryclean polyester filled sleeping bags.

Don't wash down bags with harsh detergents.

Don't pick up a wet down product without adequately supporting it.
Do air and fluff sleeping bags after each use.
Do store sleeping bags flat, on hangers, or in large porous sacks.
Do sponge clean the shell of your sleeping bag occasionally.
Do wash your sleeping bag when it gets dirty.

Tip: You can get along surprisingly well in summer without a sleeping bag if you fold a blanket or two in the manner illustrated in Figure C-5. You can also increase the warmth of any station-wagon size sleeping bag by applying the procedures outlined in Figure C-6.

Sleeping Pads, Air Mattresses, And Sleeping Systems

Background: Toddlers and teenagers can get along quite nicely without a foam pad or air mattress, but these items are a must for most adults. In general, air mattresses are much more comfortable than foam pads, but they are cold to sleep on and they frequently fail. For this reason, most expert campers choose open or closed cell foam pads over more traditional air mattresses.

Air mattresses: Except for car camping, the traditional single-valved air mattress is extinct. Such mattresses require too much time to inflate and deflate to be practical on backwoods trips. The most popular style air mattress for self-propelled outdoors people is the type which features multiple, replaceable plastic tubes, each of which has its own inflation valve. These air pads are less comfortable than traditional types but are more easily repaired (you just remove the punctured vinyl tube and replace it with a new one).

Except in the heat of summer, air mattresses cannot be used with down sleeping bags. Body weight compresses down to near zero thickness and air mattresses do not have sufficient insulation to make up for this loss. In fact, the circulating air in an air mattress simply moves the cold from place to place. Even thick polyester-filled sleeping bags (polyester doesn't compress as much as down) may get cold when the temperature drops below freezing.

Tip: Place a thin closed-cell foam pad on top of an air mattress for the ultimate in warmth and comfort.

Closed cell foam pads: You can choose "Ensolite" (PVC),

"Volarafoam" (polyethylene) or EVA (ethyl-vinyl-acetate), or a number of "mix'n match" types. EVA is so superior to other closed cell foams that it defies comparison. EVA is unaffected by sunlight, heat, and most solvents. It is almost immune to abrasion. At this writing, it is available only in a reflective aqua-blue color. It is quite expensive and worth it.

A quarter-inch thick closed cell foam pad will provide plenty of insulation for summer (but not much comfort). For winter, you'll need *at least* a three-eighths inch thickness, more for sub-zero temperatures. Closed cell foam pads are immune to water and mild abrasion so it is not necessary to cover them with material.

Open cell foam pads: There are dozens of grades of open-cell polyurethane foam. Some foams are soft and cushy, others are highly supportive. There *is* a difference in price! Select the most supportive foam you can find (try pads in the store); avoid pads which bottom out when you roll over.

Open cell foam is delicate; it must be covered, preferably with a porous fabric which will pass insensible perspiration. Avoid covers made of waterproof nylon; you'll awaken in a pool of sweat!

Don't worry about getting your open cell foam pad wet. If you storm-proof your tent, and pack as I suggest, you won't have problems with wet gear.

Therma-Rest foam/air pad: This item is so popular (nearly every camping shop has it) that it needs no introduction. The Therma-Rest is not the only combination air-mattress/foam pad, but it was the first, and it is still the lightest, most compact, and most time-proven. Basically, the unit consists of a low density (soft and cushy) open cell foam that's sealed in an envelope of vinyl and nylon. A nickle-plated brass valve controls the air flow. Open the valve and the pad inflates itself. Close the valve to lock in the air. The result is a very comfortable, incredibly warm (suitable for sub-zero use), and surprisingly reliable mattress. It is by far the favorite sleeping pad of expert campers.

Tips

1.   Make a tough cotton cover for your Therma-Rest. This will protect it from punctures and keep it from sliding on the slippery nylon tent floor. The cotton cover will also be more comfortable to sleep on than the non-porous nylon shell of the air-pad.

2.   If your covered polyurethane-foam pad migrates across the slippery tent floor as you sleep, stabilize its bottom with a few lengths of cloth adhesive tape. The tape will provide friction to stop the sliding and will remain in place until you wash the cover.

A crinkly "space blanket" (every discount store has them), set silver side up under your pad will also prevent slippage and add considerable warmth to your sleeping system.

3.   If you find yourself sleeping on an uncomfortable incline, level out your sleeping system by placing folded clothes beneath your air mat or foam pad. You can make an intolerable sleeping situation quite bearable by this method.

Snow Glasses

Dark sunglasses are necessary to prevent snow blindness in dazzling white conditions. You can make an emergency pair by applying parallel strips of electrical or duct tape to the lenses of standard glasses. Leave a narrow horizontal slit to see through.

Snowshoes

For deep, open snow, select long slender snowshoes with high turned toes (the "Alaskan" or "Pickerel" style is best). Low toed models "plow" deep under fluffy snow and double your work output.

For crusty snow or wooded areas, a small, maneuverable shoe is best. My favorite "woods shoe" is the narrow cross-country model, which is basically a miniature version of the old Alaskan, though with a lower toe. The "Sherpa" bearpaw with its ingenius binding and integral traction device may be the best deep woods/ mountain trail shoe of all. The common Michigan/Maine pattern is a good compromise style, though its low toe makes it a poor choice for fluffy snow. No one snowshoe will do everything well!

Snowshoe bindings: Leather bindings get wet and stretch; neoprene is *much* better! The standard "Sherpa" binding is by far the most comfortable, rigid, and easiest to use of all snowshoe bindings. It features a thick neoprene toe cup with stainless steel hooks and nylon strap lacing. The outfit goes on and off in seconds! All Sherpa brand shoes come standard with this unique binding, which can be purchased separately and installed on other shoes.

Traction devices for snowshoes: Sherpa bearpaws come standard with an unusual metal traction device which keeps you upright on crusty snow and ice. These traction devices are not adaptable to other snowshoes. However, you can make a simple traction device for any snowshoe by simply winding the frame with a length of braided polypropylene rope..

Sponge

A small sponge is one of the most useful and forgotten items on a camping trip. It will clean your tent floor, remove accumulated water from your canoe or boat, dissolve mud from your boots, mop up a tent leak, and much more. A natural sponge is much more absorbent than the best synthetic.

Stoves

Camp stoves are pretty trouble-free. Most will give a life-time of good service if properly maintained. Here are some troubleshooting hints and some do's and don'ts.

Troubleshooting

Problem: FLAME SPUTTERS; STOVE WON'T REACH NORMAL OPERATING TEMPERATURE.

a)   Problem is likely due to dirt in the mechanism. Turn off the stove and pour about half the fuel out. Re-cap the tank and shake the stove vigorously for a few seconds (to dislodge the clogged dirt particle). Then pour out the gas and re-fill the stove with fresh fuel. If this doesn't work, drain the stove and force high pressure air (from an air-compressor) through the filler cap opening. If this fails, the stove must be disassembled and cleaned.

b)   The safety valve, located in the filler cap, is damaged. Squirt a small amount of liquid detergent on and around the cap and check for air bubbles. If the valve is blown, replace the filler cap.

c)   Stove needs more pressure. If additional pumping doesn't do the trick, check the leather washer on the pump stem. Lubricate the washer with oil or grease. Most of the new stoves have synthetic (plastic) pump washers which don't work as well as the old leather ones. Check the plumbing section of your hardware store. Some leather stool washers fit some stoves perfectly. Note: Stoves must be insulated from the cold ground (in sub-freezing temperatures) in order to maintain operating pressure.

d) Check for improper fuel. You cannot use lead-free automotive gasoline in "white gas" stoves. Naptha (Coleman fuel) is the cleanest burning of the stove fuels, and it is pre-filtered.

e) *For Optimus/Svea stoves that don't have pumps:* Nipple may have become enlarged by improper cleaning (a bent cleaning needle will do it). The nipple (a low cost item) must be replaced. Over-priming can burn the cotton wick and reduce its absorbent qualities. The remedy is to replace the wick — something that is best done by one who is familiar with the process.

Problem: STOVE STAYS LIT FOR ABOUT 20 SECONDS, THEN SLOWLY GOES OUT. PUMPING IT REVIVES THE FLAME.

Invariably, this is the result of a slow leak in the tank filler cap. Either the safety valve is blown or the silver solder around the filler neck has melted. Replace the pressure cap, or re-solder the neck.

Check the exact location of the pressure leak by squirting liquid detergent around the pressure cap. If the safety valve checks out okay, the gasket in the filler cap is probably at fault. Replace the age-hardened gasket with a new one.

Priming

Most white gas and kerosine stoves must be pre-heated or "primed" with gasoline or alcohol in order to bring them to sufficient temperature to vaporize raw fuel. You don't need much heat to prime a gasoline stove. On a hot day, the sun or heat from your hands may generate enough pressure to cause fuel to stream from the nipple.

Pumps do not vaporize fuel; they simply allow you to maintain greater pressure in the fuel tank, which makes the stove easier to start and maintain, especially in cold weather.

Procedure for priming pump-equipped stoves:

1.   First, clean the nipple. Most stoves have a built-in cleaning needle which is activated by giving the adjuster knob a one-quarter turn counterclockwise.

2.   Be sure the pressure cap is tight and the adjuster knob is closed. Then, pump the stove a half dozen times.

3. Crack the adjuster knob a quarter turn for about four seconds, and watch fuel stream into the spirit cup below the burner head. Do not fill the spirit cup more than one-third full of gas!

4. Close the adjuster knob and ignite the fuel in the spirit cup. While the fuel is burning, give the stove another dozen pumps. When the flame has nearly died, crack the adjuster knob to permit entrance of gas. An instant blue flame should result. Note: over-priming (too much gas in the spirit cup) wastes gas, carbons up parts, and may overheat and damage stove parts. Under-priming makes stoves difficult to light. Learn to strike a compromise.

To prime stoves that don't have pumps:

1. Clean the nipple.

2. Remove the tank filler cap and withdraw an eye-dropper full of gas from the tank. Replace the filler cap. Squirt the dropper-full of gas into the spirit cup.

3. Ignite the gas in the spirit cup. When the flame has nearly gone out, crack the adjuster knob one-fourth turn. You should see a bright blue flame.

Note: The Optimus mini-pump which is sold for use in cold weather, is unnecessary if you follow the eye-dropper method of priming. Cupping stoves in hands, as is recommended by some stove makers, is slow, unreliable, and painfully cold in chilly weather.

Stoves ... do's and don'ts

Do's

DO carry fuel only in recommended containers. Sigg aluminum liter bottles, or the original container, is recommended.

DO frequently check the temperature of your stove's fuel tank by feeling it with your hand. If the tank is too hot to hold, reduce pressure and/or pour water on the tank to cool it.

DO carry extra stove parts and tools. An extra pressure cap and leather pump washer is usually enough. Bring a small screwdriver and pliers.

DO empty the fuel in your stove after each trip. And burn the stove dry at the end of the camping season. Impurities in fuel left in stoves can cause malfunctions.

DO keep your stove protected in a rigid container when it's not in use.

Don'ts:

DON'T loosen or remove the filler cap of a gasoline stove when the stove is burning. This could result in an explosion!

DON'T re-fuel a hot stove. There may be sufficient heat still available to ignite the fumes. Be especially careful in cold weather, as gasoline vaporizes much more slowly then.

DON'T set over-size pots on stoves. Large pots reflect excessive heat back to the fuel tank which may cause overheating of the stove. Run stove at three-fourths throttle if you use oversize pots.

DON'T start or run a stove inside a tent or confined area, or any place where there is insufficient ventilation.

DON'T poke wire cleaning tools into burner jets from the outside. This pushes foreign matter into the vaporization barrel and clogs the valve.

DON'T enclose a stove with aluminum foil to increase its heat output. The stove may overheat and explode!

DON'T fill gasoline or kerosine stoves more than three-fourths full. Fuel won't vaporize if there's insufficient room for it to expand. Some stoves erupt into a ball of fire when they're over-filled.

Stuff sacks

Nylon bags with drawstring closures are useful organizers for food, clothing, and small items. Camping shops sell these bags in a variety of shapes and sizes. but you can easily sew your own from nylon taffeta (see Yard Goods, page 130) in a few minutes.

Note: Ordinary fabric shops don't usually stock waterproof nylon, but the best camping shops do.

Tents

Tent camping becomes more popular each year. Dozens of manufacturers offer literally hundreds of tent models. Getting exactly what you want is simply a matter of matching your needs to your pocket book. Here are some things to think about before you buy:

Size: Each camper needs about 7 feet by 2 1/2 feet in which to stretch out and store gear. Increase the area to 8 by 3 and you enter the realm of comfort. A 7 by 8 foot floor plan and enough room to sit fully upright is ideal for two. For auto camping, and any semi-permanent tent camp, the more space the merrier. Figure on a maximum ridge height of 5 feet. Tents which stand much taller than this blow down, even in moderate winds.

Bulk is often more important than weight. You can live with a few extra pounds, even on a go-light backpack journey, but not with a tent that won't fit in your pack. The culprit is usually the length of the tent poles. Sections longer than about 22 inches won't fit inside most packs without protruding from under the closing flap (where they may fall out and become lost). You'll find a clever method for packing tent poles on page 79.

Weight: For auto camping, any "reasonable" weight is acceptable, though veteran campers would agree that 35 pounds is tops for ease-of-handling. Self-propelled campers should select models which are no heavier than three and one-half pounds per person (thus, a three person tent should weigh no more than ten and one-half pounds). Again, overall packed size may be more important than an extra pound or two.

Wind integrity: If you camp above the treeline you need a wind-stable tent. But don't pay extra dollars for this feature if your activities are confined to the deep forest. Good wind tents tend to be low and dog-housy, not what you want for enjoying the day in an all day storm. Any tent of reasonable design will withstand winds to 35 miles per hour if you know how to rig it (see *Stormproofing your tent*, at the end of this section).

Rain-proofing: Not all tents are equally rainproof. Tents designed in southern California tend to minimize the importance of rain protection while east coast designs go to extraordinary lengths to ensure it. Of course, there are many exceptions. If rain-proofing ranks high on your list, your best bet is to avoid the advertising hype and pitch of the salesperson, and instead, personally check out these important "rain features."

1. *Bathtub floor:* The most stormproof tents have waterproof floors which wrap at least 6 inches up the sidewalls before they are sewn to the tent body. This eliminates perimeter seams for water to drip on ... and leak through. You can, of course, waterproof seams (and you should) with liquid sealant (glue), but this is not foolproof. Some very exotic tents (notably, domes) necessarily feature lots of perimeter seams which must be continually waterproofed to prevent leakage. *Don't depend on chemical seam sealants to keep you dry in a rain; opt instead for "good design!"*

2. The waterproof rainfly should cover the porous tent canopy completely and stake right to the ground. There should be no air spaces into which rain can blow. An inch or two gap here is permissible, though contact with the ground is best.

3. Check the corner floor seams (even bathtub floors necessarily have corner seams). The fly must cover these *completely*. Partially, is not good enough. Examine the tent corners from every possible angle. Could wind blow aside the fly and allow rain to

drip on seams? If so, don't buy the tent, no matter how good it otherwise looks.

4.   There should be substantial awnings over doors and windows. Zippered flaps are not sufficient!

5.   All exposed zippers must be covered with rain flaps. check these flaps carefully. Could wind blow them aside and allow rain to contact the zippers? If so, you're in for a drenching in the first big storm.

6.   Finally, the tent should have a vestibule (an integral or add-on extension that attaches to the front of the tent). Vestibules provide a protected place to store gear, out of the main sleeping compartment. Equally important, they waterproof the door end of the tent by sealing off zippers, eaves and seams. And they improve the aerodynamics of the tent by presenting a sharp wedge-shape to the wind. The most weatherproof tent I've used is the three-person Cannondale Aroostook, (Cannondale, Inc., 9 Brookside Place, Georgetown, CT 06829.) which features a built-in vestibule at each end.

A review of tent styles

A-frame: Oldest of the tent shapes and still one of the best. A-frame tents shed wind and water effectively and they're relatively inexpensive to manufacture. Inexpensive models feature a single I-pole at each end while more elaborate designs have two "vee" poles or an aluminum exoskeleton. A-frames are definitely not "high-tech," but they're well suited to most kinds of camping, from desert hikes to ski treks. This is the most versatile tent design and best value for the dollar.

Domes provide more interior space for the fabric use, than any other tent shape. Domes are the most delightful of all tents to be in; on rough ground you can switch around to find a place that's comfortable. And these tents provide room for all the occupants to sit upright without touching the tent canopy. These tents are basically self-supporting; they go up easily on sand, snow or rock.

However, there are some real negatives. Unless there is a tunnel entrance or awning, rain pours in every time you go in or out! Domes also require extensive guying in strong winds (you'll have stakes and guylines everywhere!) to remain upright. And, they have an incredible number of floor level and perimeter seams which must be waterproofed. They also tend to be rather time-consuming to erect, especially in high winds.

In short, domes are best at home in dry climates where high winds are infrequent. Most domes are lousy rain tents!

Geodesic domes are the Cadillac of dome tents. They are supported by a strong, faceted framework of tubular aluminum. The best geodesic tents are so strong you can sit on them without distorting their shape. Some models have been proven on the slopes of Mount Everest and the high arctic. Geodesic domes are strong, reliable tents. They are quite expensive and not very versatile for the kind of camping most people do. Like conventional domes, they are not well adapted to rainy climates.

Tepees: The Indian knew what he was doing when he invented the tepee. No other tent of comparable size sheds wind and water as effectively, is as cool in summer, as warm in winter, and generally as versatile. The Indian tepee is a marvel on any terrain.

The modern nylon tepee is a far cry from its skin-covered ancestor. Three aluminum poles provide support and a removable polyurethane-coated fly keeps out the weather. Entry is a zippered door or traditional hole. Tepees are roomy and pleasant; like domes, you can sleep in any direction.

However, they require *lots* of stakes to erect, and most have three-quarter length (cap) flies which allow rain to splash in. Like domes, they lack awnings, so rain follows you in. In all, tepees are best suited to relatively dry open areas.

Tunnels are marvelously wind-stable tents which are best at home in the snow-swept mountains. Low-to-the-ground tunnels are the most wind stable of all tents, but they're terribly confining.

Self-supporting tents: Any tent design can be made self-supporting if it is rigged with a tubular exoskeleton and shock-cord suspension system. Note that self-supporting tents remain "freestanding" only if there is no wind — a fierce storm will send any unanchored tent reeling across the countryside. The real advantage of self-supporting tents is that they require fewer stakes to erect than traditional U-stake 'em models. But these tents do require staking … nearly always!

Tent poles: The best tent poles are made from three-quarter inch diameter tempered aluminum. Solid fiberglass poles break instantly; hollow ones last a day or two. "High-tech" composite poles and flimsy aluminum poles may go a full season before they bend, break or splinter. And don't let tent salesmen convince you otherwise!

Shock-cording keeps pole sections together and adds some strength. All the best tent poles are shock-corded.

Tip: Tent poles will be less apt to jam together if you polish the joints (a one time effort) with 400 grit sandpaper then wipe them with a silicone cloth.

Tip: Remedy for stuck pole sections: Heat the joint lightly in the flame of your trail stove. The joint will expand and the poles will part easily.

Tent stakes: Avoid stakes which must be pounded in with a hammer. Eight inch long aluminum staples or pins are the best choice, except in sand or snow where a greater bite is required.

Special stakes are really unnecessary for camping on snow or sand. Conventional aluminum staples can be buried, or guylines wound about wooden sticks then buried. Tin can lids (with the edges peened in for safety) make good snow stakes (run the guy lines through holes in the center and bury the lids).

Six inch long aluminum nails (available at every hardware store) make excellent low cost tent stakes.

Stormproofing your tent

1.   Waterproof the seams of a new tent. I prefer to use "Thompson's Water Seal" rather than glues which crack, peel, and absorb dirt. Apply TWS sparingly with a foam varnish brush. Two applications per seam side are recommended. This product is also useful for waterproofing maps, journals and hats.

2.   Attach loops of shock-cord or bands cut from inner tubes to all stake points and guylines. Rubber bands take up the wind stress normally reserved for seams and fittings. Even a badly sewn, poorly reinforced tent can be used in severe weather if it's rigged with shock-cords.

3.   Tents which are completely self-supporting, like the Eureka Timberline, will blow down in a gale if you don't run one or more guylines off the peak at each end. For best results in a severe storm, run *three* guylines off each end, as illustrated in Figure T-1.

118

Figure T-1. Stormproofing the tent:

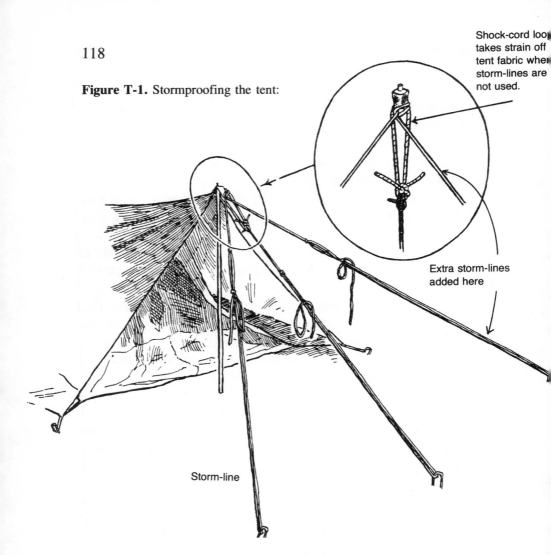

Shock-cord loop takes strain off tent fabric when storm-lines are not used.

Extra storm-lines added here

Storm-line

4.   Place a four or six-mil thick plastic groundcloth *inside* your tent. Make the groundcloth large enough so it "flows" a few inches up the tent walls. If your tent springs a leak, water will be trapped under the groundsheet and you'll stay dry. *Do not* place the ground cloth outside the tent floor (exception — in winter to prevent the floor from freezing to the ground). Surface water may become trapped between the ground sheet and floor and be pressure wicked (from body weight) through the floor seams. You'll really have a sponge party if this happens!

Contrary to the claims of tent-makers, you don't need a ground cloth under your tent floor to protect it from abrasion. Holes in tent floors usually develop from *inside* the tent. If you don't believe this, begin a trip with a new plastic ground-sheet inside your tent, then count the holes it accumulates with each day of use. Old beliefs die hard!

5.   If a seam looks weak, it probably is. Reinforce stress points with heavy carpet thread and nylon webbing.

6.   A-frame tents should have *at least* three stakes along each side to ensure adequate security in high winds. If the hem of your tent looks like it needs additional stake lines, add them.

7.   You can make tents with three-quarter length flies suitable for use in rough weather if you extend the sides of the fly to ground level. Matching material can be obtained from the tent manufacturer and many outdoor stores (see section on YARD GOODS, page 130).

Tips: Shock-cord all tent poles. Shock-cording kits are available at most camp shops.

Color-code non shock-corded pole sections and wands for easy assembly. It's frustrating to look for a "center ridge section" or "spreader bar" in failing light. Colored plastic tape sticks to poles better than paint.

Tents with self-supporting frameworks depend heavily on brass hooks, pins and spring clips for attachment to the poles. Be careful that this hardware doesn't abrade the nylon fabric when you roll or stuff these tents.

Store your tent in an *oversize* stuff sack. The ones that come with tents are usually too small. A snug fitting sack looks nice in the store, but the tent won't fit when it's watersoaked and mud-caked.

Be sure your tent is thoroughly dry before you pack it away. Wet nylon probably won't mildew, but polyurethane coatings will. If you've ever seen a tent floor whose polyurethane coating has peeled off, you know the owner packed it away wet.

Tips on packing your tent will be found on page 79.

Care and cleaning of tents

Canvas tents: Sweep 'em out hose 'em down with water, and let 'em sun dry until they are bone dry. Don't use soaps or detergents to clean cotton tents as these products will remove the water-proofing compounds.

Tip: You can restore the water-repellency to small sections of cotton tents by rubbing a bar of paraffin across the fibers. Heat from the sun will melt the paraffin and the cotton fibers will absorb it.

Canvas tents should be stored in porous bags, well away from moisture or concrete.

Nylon tents should be thoroughly washed at the end of each camping season. Soak the tent for 30 minutes or so in a tub full of luke warm water and mild detergent. Tent manufacturers wisely suggest you avoid use of detergents and chemical solvents as these products may dissolve waterproof coatings. However, sparing use of these products remove abrasive dirt, which is your tent's greatest enemy. Sponge troublesome spots with detergent. Tree sap may be removed with a *very small* amount of gasoline. Don't overdo it though; gasoline is very hard on polyurethane coatings.

Dry nylon tents thoroughly before you put them away. Sustained exposure to ultraviolet light saps strength from nylon fabrics. A nylon tent may lose half or more of its strength in a single season if it's continually exposed to sunlight. *Do* sun-dry and air your tent regularly, but don't overdo it!

Nylon tent lines age harden and lose strength. They should be replaced occasionally.

Tip: Attach a tiny brass hook to the lanyard of your flashlight so you can clip it to a ridge loop inside your tent.

Tip: Sew a D-ring or nylon loop inside your tent at each end of the ridge. A length of parachute cord strung between the D-rings makes a handy "clothesline" for light items. Damp socks will dry surprisingly well if hung overnight from the ridge cord.

Tip: A small candle lantern will raise interior tent temperatures by 10 degrees or more, and eliminate much dampness.

Tent-Site: How To Cope With A Bad One!

The camping literature is rich with advice on how to choose a good campsite. Requirements generally include high flat ground with good drainage, a south-facing slope (so you can enjoy the morning sun), and an open vista so a welcome breeze will blow away bothersome insects. In reality, a rank novice can tell a good tent spot when he or she sees one. Everyone knows enough not to pitch a tent on bumpy ground, on a rock face, or in a depression. However, most camping today is carefully regulated, and some programmed sites are downright awful. In most cases, you'll have to accept the inadequacies of the place and try to make the best of it. Here are some suggestions as to how to do just that:

1.   Always use a ground cloth *inside* your tent. Storm-proof your tent as suggested in the previous section.

2.   Know the shortcomings of your tent and correct them. For example, the most weather-vulnerable portion of any tent is the door end, where zippers and seams come together. A vestibule will solve this problem instantly, however, not all tents come so equipped. If the ground slopes, pitch the tent with the weather-vulnerable end *down hill*, so ground water will run away from the seams rather than on to them.

3.   If the site drainage is bad, and there are a number of tents in your party, pitch each tent far enough away from its neighbor so that tent roofs won't funnel water on to nearby tents. Closely spaced tents act as gutters in a heavy rain!

4.   Please do not "improve" the lay of the ground by attacking it with a hatchet and Rambo knife. Instead, use foam pads or air-mattresses. Level your sleeping system by placing additional clothing beneath your trail bed.

5.   There will not always be trees available from which to rig cooking flies. An extra set of collapsible tent poles will provide anchor points for tarps.

6.   If, despite all your precautions, a heavy rain threatens to wipe you out, create water diversion bars by placing logs alongside your tent's perimeter. The logs will function much like the erosion control bars used for trail maintenance. After the rain, return logs to the forest so you'll leave no trace of your presence.

7.   An anti-rain dance or thoughtful plea to the Great Spirit will sometimes cause the brunt of a storm to bypass a bad tent spot.

Wanigans

Background: Wanigans are rigid boxes which were commonly used in the fur trade to carry hard goods like knives, guns and axes that would be uncomfortable in a standard soft pack. Modern campers can use wanigans for the same purpose. For auto camping, nothing beats a well organized "camp kitchen," which has compartments for tin cans, utensils and soft goods. Most commercial models have a plywood lid that doubles as both work area and cutting board. You can get detailed plans for making a camp kitchen from many scout and "Y" camps.

Smaller hard packs are handy for canoe camping, picnicking, berry picking, and anywhere you need a strong, rigid container. The traditional hard pack for canoeing is the Maine pack basket, which is available by mail from L. L. Bean. (L.L. Bean, Inc. Freeport, Maine 04033) If you place a woven ash basket into a waterproof sack (the army surplus waterproof clothes bag is just the right size), then set this unit into a tailored backpack, you'll have a strong, watertight container that's comfortable to carry.

Tip: Make a number of narrow fabric pockets and attach these to the inside rim of your packbasket. Store sunglasses, fillet knife, and other small items in these handy organizers.

A less expensive solution is to nest a cheap rectangular plastic trash container inside a soft pack. This outfit will protect all your breakables.

A medium sized plastic ice-chest (cooler) can also be pressed into service as a wanigan. It will be easier to carry if you strap it to a tubular aluminum pack frame.

Figure W-1. The E.M. Wanigan box:

You'll find aluminum and plastic wanigans at some camping stores. They are quite expensive. Best of the lot is the E. M. Wanigan, (E.M. Wanigan, 10411 Kelman Court North, Stillwater, MN 55082.) which boasts 5,200 cubic inches of space and comes outfitted with padded shoulder straps and an optional hip belt. The "Wanigan box" is absolutely watertight and is so strong you can stand on it. A plastic dish pan and tray set is available for those who prefer this convenience.

Water Treatment

There are few places in North America where you can safely drink water from a lake or stream. And conditions don't seem to be improving. Water quality — and just plain availability of water — is now the major environmental concern. Unless you always camp where the quality of drinking water is guaranteed, you're well advised to carry in your water or treat it by one of the following methods.

Field methods of water treatment

1.   *Boiling:* Most organisms are killed instantly when water reaches the boiling point. Almost none can survive a five minute boil. Despite the availability of sophisticated mechanical filters and chemicals, "boiling" is the most reliable — and preferred — method of treating drinking water.

2.   *Filtration:* A number of mechanical filters are available at camping stores, but most are not very practical, especially for use with large groups. If you opt for filtration, choose a large capacity unit whose pores will remove the smallest infectious agents. A 0.4 micron grid size will trap most microbes. Be sure the filter is easily cleaned (or replaced). Best field unit at this writing is the Swiss made "Katadyn," which has a 0.2 micron pore size and costs about 150 dollars. (Katadyn filters may be mail ordered from Indiana Camp Supply, P.O. Box 211, Hobart, Indiana 46342.)

3.   *Chemical treatment:* "Halazone" tablets are an old standby which has been available in corner drugstores for years. If you use Halazone, take an unopened bottle on each trip. The product loses considerable strength when exposed to air and heat. Halazone tablets release chlorine, which is carcinogenic.

Chlorine: Liquid chlorine bleach with four to six percent available chlorine may be used to purify water. Use two drops of bleach per quart of clear water and four drops per quart of cold or cloudy water. Let treated water stand for 30 minutes before using. You should be able to smell the chlorine gas. If not, repeat the dosage and let it stand another 15 minutes before using. If the water is very cold or cloudy, let it stand overnight before using.

Note: None of the chemicals work very well in cold, cloudy water. Under these conditions, your best bet is to *boil* your water!

Tip: You can sterilize your camp dishes by simply adding a splash of chlorine bleach to the final rinse water.

Iodine: Place six grams of iodine (your pharmacist will weigh it out for you) in a one-ounce amber bottle. Fill the bottle with water. The iodine crystals will dissolve until a saturated solution results, then no more crystals will dissolve.

Sterilize a quart canteen of water by pouring about half (the amount isn't critical) the iodine solution into the canteen. Let the canteen stand at least 30 minutes before drinking. Allow additional time for cold or cloudy water.

Recharge the iodine bottle with fresh water after each use. Only a small amount of iodine will dissolve from the crystals each time, so you may continue to use the "iodine decant bottle" dozens of times until no more crystals are visible.

Caution: Do not allow any iodine crystals to enter your canteen. Large doses of iodine can be fatal! (Iodine is a rather heavy metal and is quite visible in solution, so you'll have no trouble seeing the crystals or containing them in your bottle.)

You may also treat your water with a commercial tablet that releases iodine. "Potable Aqua" (sold nearly everywhere) is highly recommended.

A two percent tincture of iodine solution may also be used to purify water. Use six to eight drops of iodine per quart of drinking water. Let the chemical work for at least 30 minutes before you drink the water. Double the dosage and working time if the water is cold or cloudy.

Note: Products which release chlorine will not destroy cysts of the *Giardia* parasite (see description of *Giardia*, below) under all conditions. If you suspect contamination by this parasite, *boil* your water! Authorities generally agree that compounds which release iodine are more reliable than those which emit chlorine.

Where not to get your drinking water

1.　Go well away from the shoreline to get drinking water. If you're camping at a spot frequented by man or animals, go *upstream* of the source to get water. On lakes, go a minimum of 150 feet from shore, and the farther (and deeper) the better.

Tip: Place a rock in your largest cooking pot and lower it deep into the lake with a long rope. Work the bucket up and down like a yo-yo to guarantee good exchange of water. Water taken 20 feet or more below the lake surface is apt to be most trustworthy.

2.　Avoid water which has a greenish color. The green tinge indicates the presence of algae, which attracts microorganisms.

Tan-colored water, however, is usually safe. Invariably, this color suggests natural run-off tannic acid from adjacent conifer stands (quite common throughout the upper midwest).

3.　Take your drinking water from fast moving areas; avoid

backwaters, stagnant areas, and eddies which are breeding places for microorganisms.

4. Never drink any water which has been contaminated by wastes from a paper mill. Instead, secure your water from incoming streams or springs.

5. Don't take water near beaver dams or lodges. Beaver are the favored host of *Giardia lamblia*, a small protozoan that may cause severe discomfort. Giardia enters a water supply through the feces of the host. Its cyst can survive up to two months in 46 degree Fahrenheit water, and up to one month in 70 degree water!

The infection carried by the organism is called "giardiasis" and it's characterized by severe diarrhea, cramps, nausea and vomiting. Incubation time is one to two weeks, though some people have gone as long as two months without getting sick. If untreated, the disease may go on for years!

Giardiasis is usually diagnosed by stool examination, which is not always reliable. Most physicians just haven't had enough experience with the disease to correctly diagnose it. As a result, many victims suffer for months before they get the help they need. Not everyone who is exposed to the Giardia parasite comes down with the disease. Indeed, most people are simply carriers.

Weather Forecasting

Background: Every outdoors person should have a basic understanding of weather phenomena and be able to make reasonably accurate short term weather predictions. Some campers take forecasting quite seriously; they arm themselves with min/max thermometers, barometers, cloud charts and weather tables. Whether or not this paraphernalia will improve your short range forecasts is debatable. After all, primitive man is right on target more than 80 percent of the time, simply by looking at the sky, sensing the wind, and "feeling" the weather. You can approximate this enviable success rate by applying these time-proven principles:

1. "Red sky at night, sailor's delight; Red sky in the morning, sailor take warning." Translation: A red morning sky indicates possible rain that day; a red evening sky suggests the next day will be clear. The color difference relates to the reflective value of the low lying cloud cover.

2.   Check the grass, tent, canoe bottom, or whatever, for the presence of dew in late evening or early morning. A heavy dew at either of these times usually suggests 8 to 12 hours of good weather.

3.   Watch the smoke from your campfire. If it hangs low (a function of low pressure) to the ground, rain is on the way. If it rises high into a nice vertical column (high pressure), count on good weather.

3.   Check out the air bubbles in your coffee cup. They'll ring the edges of the cup when a low pressure (rain) system sets in.

4.   You can sometimes smell a coming storm, as the low pressure allows methane (swamp gas) to rise and drift with the currents. In boggy areas, the odor is quite pronounced.

5.   "When the peacock loudly bawls, there'll be both rain and squalls." Translation: Birds sing loudly just before a storm.

6.   Geese and seagulls won't usually fly just before a storm. Low pressure air is thin and it's hard for them to get airborne.

7.   The ears of many animals are sensitive to low pressure. Wolves will howl before a storm. Dogs will become nervous and emit howls or howl-like sounds.

8.   To determine the distance of a lightning strike, count the seconds between the flash and the thunder boom. Divide by five and you'll have your answer in miles.

9.   Noises all become louder and more vibrant just before a rain, because the sound is reflected and magnified by the low clouds. The croaking of frogs, yodel of loons, etc., will echo loudly if rain is imminent.

10.   Be alert for changes in wind direction. Storms are whirlpools of wind that rotate counterclockwise in the northern hemisphere (remember your high school science?). The adage, "Wind from the south, brings rain in its mouth," is the keystone here, as the wind which precedes a storm usually blows from the south. Counterclockwise wind shifts therefore usually bring rain, while clockwise movements indicate fair weather. You can keep these directional changes straight by remembering the rhymes ...

"Wind from the east brings weather that's a beast." (Suggests a counterclockwise wind shift from south to east, east to north, etc.)

"Wind from the west brings weather that's best." (Suggests a clockwise wind shift from south to west, north to east, etc.)

11.   Most everyone knows that frogs emerge from the water just before a storm and croak their fool heads off. Frogs breathe partly through their skin (which must be kept moist), so when the humidity rises just before a storm, they climb ashore and sing happily.

12.   If you're a canoeist you know that about 8-12 hours before a storm, mosquitoes and black flies begin to swarm and bite more than usual. and up to two hours before the storm they quit biting altogether.

13.   Check out the rainbow: A heavy red may mean more rain; vibrant rich blue suggests clear skies ahead.

14.   Here's an old "down east" proverb: "Filly tails make lofty ships wear low sails." Translation: Thin, hair-like clouds forecast rain within the day. These "filly tails" are really streaks of ice thrown skyward by the rising air of a coming storm.

15.   A "mackerel sky" (tiny scale-like clouds that resemble a mackerel's back), just 24 hours dry. Translation: Expect rain within the next day!

16.   Any fireflies around? When rain approaches, these little insects light up the woods in gay profusion, according to the rhyme: "When the little glow bug lights his lamp, the air around is surely damp."

17.   Listen for the rustle of leaves as the wind precedes the storm.

18.   If you can't see the sharp points on a half moon, rain may be in the offing. Translation: Low clouds and haze distort sharp images.

19.   Bright, twinkling stars usually indicate high altitude winds which may be bringing in a storm.

20.   There's a good chance that foul weather (rain or snow) will fall within three days of a new moon phase.

21.   "The weather out west had best be best, for tomorrow will bring it to you to test!" This means that in all likelihood, the weather system to your west will be at your location tomorrow.

22.   In summer, a "sun-dog" or halo around the sun, generally predicts the coming of rain. Sun-dogs are caused by sunlight streaming through the ice particles of high clouds. A halo around the moon may also indicate approaching rain.

23. "Evening fog will not burn soon, but morning fog will burn before high noon." Invariably, a fog-borne day will become perfectly clear (an ideal day) by noon.

24. "Short notice, soon it will pass. Long notice, expect it to last." Watch the clouds, If they take several days to build, a prolonged rain is usually in the offing. If the storm system builds suddenly, it will probably pass quickly.

25. And of course, everyone knows: "Rain before seven, dry by eleven."

Yard Goods

Cotton and nylon yard goods are available for the home manufacture and repair of camping equipment. Most high quality camp shops carry some yard goods and repair items. CAMPMOR, Inc., P.O. Box 999, Paramus, New Jersey 07653-0999, is a very complete mail order source for the most popular fabrics and repair items. Here's how these fabrics differ:

Cotton

Cotton is a marvelous material for large, semi-permanent tents and for any application that requires breathability and durability. Military tents are still constructed from canvas duck, as are most of the high grade wall tents you see in western hunting camps.

Canvas breathes as it sheds water, which means tents made of this fabric are wonderfully comfortable (no condensation) in wet weather. Worn canvas is easily restored to "waterproof condition" by painting on chemicals which can be purchased in most hardware stores. Mending the damaged polyurethane coatings on nylon fabrics is at best, difficult.

Cotton has a non-skid surface, a nice soft "hand," and it feels good against the skin. It's ideal as a covering for foam sleeping

130

pads and seat and boat cushions, for tent and tool bags, and hats. A cotton-poplin parka is luxurious and will ward off quite a shower if treated with water repellent chemicals. Cotton fabrics retain water-repellents much more willingly than do nylon materials.

Army duck is the strongest and heaviest (and most expensive!) of the cotton fabrics. It is woven so that each warp yarn passes over (or under) a single filling yarn (similar to those loop pot holders you made as a child). "Duck" is available in weights from 7 to 15 ounces per square yard. The army prefers 12-15 ounce fabrics for their heavy truck tarps and bivouac tents, but 7 to 8 ounce weights are better for family campers. Army duck is the king of cotton tent fabrics.

Twill is woven so that each warp yarn passes over two or more filling yarns. It's less strong than duck and is used mostly to make military uniforms. It's tough stuff and it weighs about 8 ounces per square yard.

Drill is a three-leaf twill made from fairly coarse yarns. It's more loosely woven than duck and less expensive. The cheapest canvas tents are often made from drill.

Cotton-poplin is a tightly woven fabric that's produced by using yarns which are heavier and more coarse than the warp yarns. Poplin comes in weights of 4 to 11 ounces per square yard. Some of the best family sized wall tents are woven from five and one-half ounce fabric.

Egyptian, Pima, and Supima cotton: Exyptian cotton has the longest fibers of all cottons and it makes into the strongest and silkiest yarn. It is by far the most luxurious fabric for the interior shells of sleeping bags; no other material feels better against the skin. "Pima" cotton was developed by U.S. growers to compete with the Exyptian product, and it is nearly as good. "Supima" is the top of the Pima crop. Tightly woven high grade cotton isn't used much in its pure form anymore (it's very expensive). However, it is a marvelous material for sleeping bags, windshells and summer shirts.

Cotton ventile was originally developed by the British to keep downed RAF fliers from freezing in the North Sea. It is so tightly woven that it will repel a shower for 20 minutes or more without the aid of chemical water repellents. Until the advent of Gore-Tex,

all the best parkas in the world were made from ventile. Unfortunately, this fabric is heavy when dry, heavier when wet, very
expensive and difficult to find. It is a wonderfully luxurious material.

Nylon fabrics

Nylon needs no introduction. It is used in everything from
tents to boots. Nylon is strong, light, and relatively inexpensive.
On the negative side, it degrades badly in ultra-violet light, and it
stretches considerably when wet. It also shrinks over the years.

Taffeta is a flat woven fabric that weighs between 2.5 and 3.5
ounces per square yard. Taffeta is more prone to tear than rip-stop,
but it has greater resistance to abrasion, the reason why most tent
flies and floors are made of this material.

Polyurethane-coated nylon taffeta is the fabric of choice for
lightweight rain gear, stuff sacks, and backpack tarps. Uncoated
(porous) taffeta is a popular fabric for garments. Uncoated taffeta
has no water repellency.

Rip-stop has a gridwork of heavy threads woven in at quarter-
inch intervals to increase fabric strength. It weighs 1.5-2.0 ounces
per square yard. Rip-stop is widely used for lightweight tent
canopies, sleeping bag shells and wind garments. Coated rip-stop
makes a nice lightweight rain tarp.

Vinyl-coated-nylon is a heavyweight plastic-coated nylon used
largely for heavy-duty tent floors and tarps. It's much stronger and
more resistant to abrasion than coated taffeta but its vinyl coating
may soften or peel if it is exposed to heavy doses of harsh solvents,
such as those used in some insecticides.

Polyethylene-coated polyethylene is a tough polyethylene fabric with a polyethylene plastic coating on both sides. The material
is mildew-proof and is commonly used for heavy-duty tent floors
and tarps. Both vinyl-coated nylon and polyethylene-coated
polyethylene are much more dimensionally stable (less wet-stretch/
dry-shrinkage) than polyurethane-coated nylon.

Cordura is the toughest nylon of all. It resists abrasion and
puncture far better than any other fabric of equal weight. Many of
the best backpacks are made from it and it's widely used in the
manufacture of lightweight hiking boots. However, heavy-weight
cordura does not accept waterproofing compounds very well. Invar-

iably, pinholes (which you can see when the fabric is held to a strong light) of untreated nylon remain which will admit water.

Coated oxford cloth* (which weighs about 6 ounces per square yard) is a strong, absolutely watertight fabric used in the manufacture of lightweight packsacks. This is the same stuff that Eureka uses for the flooring in their outfitter Timberline tents. It is the best material I've found for making fabric splash covers for canoes.

Blends

Sixty/forty cloth (60 percent cotton/40 percent nylon) is woven with nylon threads in one direction and cotton in the other. The nylon supplies strength, the cotton provides water repellency and a luxurious feel. A lot of great mountain parkas are built from 60/40 cloth.

Sixty-five/thirty-five cloth: Cotton and dacron yarns are blended together then woven into the garment. Threads of each yarn run in both directions. This fabric is supposed to be more water-repellent and have greater strength than 60/40 cloth.

There are also a number of exotic blends which feature cotton, dacron, and nylon in varying weaves and amounts. Generally, the higher the nylon content, the stronger, lighter and less water-repellent the garment. More cotton and dacron means a softer "hand," higher water repellency, and heavier weight. In practice, the differences between these similar fabrics are relatively insignificant.

*(All these nylon fabrics can be had with or without waterproof coatings. Weight and cost of the fabrics will vary depending upon type and amount of coating applied.)

Appendix A

Glossary Of Common Camping Terms

agonic line: a line of zero compass declination, along which the compass needle "points" to both true and magnetic north.

A-frame tent: an inverted V-shaped tent with one or two poles at each end.

anorak: a shell parka that goes on over-the-head. Anoraks have a chestlength zipper or snaps. They conserve heat better than a full-zip parka.

Arkansas stone: a medium-hard mineral stone used for putting a fine edge on knives.

azimuth: commonly used to indicate a directional bearing in degrees or mils. Technically, "azimuth" relates direction to one (or a fraction of one) of the 360 degrees of the compass rose. A *bearing* (often used synonymously with azimuth) relates direction to the north or south cardinal point. Example: an azimuth of 330 degrees equals a bearing of N 30° W. An azimuth of 160° equals a bearing of S 20° E. etc.

135

baffle: fabric panels sewn to the inner and outer shell of a sleeping bag. Baffles keep the insulation in place. Down bags must be baffled. Most synthetic bags feature quilted insulation.

bannock: the traditional trail bread. Usually made in a skillet by a combination of frying and reflective baking.

bathtub floor: a tent floor which wraps six inches or more up the side-walls of the tent before it is sewn. This construction eliminates perimeter seams at ground level which can leak in rain.

Bean boots: slang for "Maine hunting shoe," the leather top/rubber bottom boots invented by Leon Bean.

bearing: a compass direction (see azimuth).

billy can: a straight-sided cooking pot with a wire bail.

bivouac: technically a temporary encampment. Modern usage connotes an emergency or bush camp — made where no other camp has stood.

blousing bands: elastic bands used by the military to secure pant leg bottoms around boots. Blousing bands are useful for sealing trouser legs against mosquitoes and black flies.

breathable: refers to the porosity of fabrics. Breathable materials are not waterproof.

bug jacket: a fabric mesh jacket that's impregnated with insect repellent.

cagoule: a waterproof, ankle length (over- the-head) parka used by mountaineers for bivouacking. Cagoules have well tailored hoods and drawstring hems. The wearer pulls his legs inside, draws the hem tight, and "outlasts" the elements.

canopy: the (usually porous) roof of a tent. Not to be confused with the waterproof tent "fly."

cap-fly: A three-quarter length tent fly. Tents with cap flies are not as weatherproof as are those with full-length flies.

catenary cut: the natural curve formed by a rope that's tightly strung between two trees. A tent which has a catenary cut rigs tighter (less sidewall sag) than one without catenary cut. Catenary cut is a feature of the best tents.

chute cord: slang for parachute cord.

contour lines: thin brown lines on maps which connect points of equal elevation.

cord-lock: A spring-loaded nylon clamp used to secure the drawstring closures of stuff sacks.

crash out: to bushwack out of a forested area, to a trail, road or meadow.

Croakies: brand name of a very popular elastic security strap for eye glasses.

cruiser compass: a needle compass which has the numbers on the dial reversed (running counterclockwise rather than clockwise) to permit reading bearings in the same plane as the observer's eye. Cruiser compasses are still used by some professionals, but there are better choices for campers. The outdated design of these instruments dates to the 19th century.

declination: the difference between true or geographic north and magnetic north. Declination (also called "variation" by mariners) is expressed in degrees east or west of the agonic line.

DEET: slang for diethyl-meta-toluamide, the active ingredient in most insect repellents.

diamond stone: a type of man-made sharpening stone which contains powdered diamonds. Diamond stones are lubricated with water (not cutting oil). They remove metal much faster than traditional oilstones.

differential cut: the inner shell of a sleeping bag is cut smaller than the outer shell, to produce a Thermos bottle effect. The merits of this construction are still being argued by equipment freaks.

dining fly: an overhead tarp (fly) used for protection from rain. Usually erected just before mealtimes, hence the descriptive name.

double-wall tent: a tent with a wall that's two layers thick. All modern nylon tents are built this way and feature a breathable taffeta canopy (inner wall) and a watertight rip-stop fly (outer wall). Double-wall canvas tents are sometimes used in winter (with a sheepherder stove) to conserve heat.

draft tube: a down-filled tube that runs the length of a sleeping bag zipper — prevents cold air from filtering through the zipper teeth.

dropped-point knife: The favored style for hunting knives — the point is centered (similar to a spear-point) on the blade. Dropped-point knives are ideal for skinning game animals but are not the most suitable style for camp knives.

Dutch oven: A unique oven which consists of a heavywalled pot and cover with a large retaining rim. Coals from the fire are placed on top of the pot lid and the affair is set into the hot ashes. Heat from the top does most of the baking.

Duluth pack: a voluminous envelope style (usually, canvas) pack popular with canoeists.

EVA (ethyl-vinyl-acetate): Strongest, most resiliant, and most expensive of the closed-cell foams. EVA makes an excellent trail mattress.

fanny pack: A small zippered nylon pack that's attached to a waist-belt.

ferrule: the metal sleeve that's attached to the pole sections of fiberglass tent poles. Ferrules form a joint between pole sections.

filling power (of down): Same as "loft". It's the thickness of a sleeping bag lying flat and fluffed. Generally speaking, the greater the "loft" of a sleeping bag, the warmer it will be.

fisherman's shirt: (see cagoule). Same as a cagoule only calf-length and without drawstring hem.

flat-fell seam: overlapping construction; the seam goes through four layers of material.

floating dial compass: the compass needle is part of the numbered compass dial, which rotates as a unit. This allows the instrument to be read in the same plane as the eye of the user. Some styles are very accurate.

foam pad: a sleeping mattress made of either open-cell or closed-cell foam.

frame pack: a pack with an exterior aluminum or fiber framework.

frost liner: A detachable inner "roof" for a tent that absorbs moisture which might condense, freeze, and drop on sleeping occupants. Frost liners are made from cotton or cotton/polyester fabric and are needed only in below freezing conditions.

fuel bottle: traditionally refers to "Sigg" aluminum bottles, which are used for the storage of gasoline and kerosine.

gators: nylon anklets (usually with side zippers) used by skiers and mountaineers. Gators prevent snow from getting in your boot tops, and they add extra warmth.

Giardia: the causative pathogen of "giardiasis."

giardiasis: a waterborne disease carried by the protozoan "Giardia." Giardia is commonly carried by beaver. Incubation time is one to two weeks. The pathogen is very hardy. See text description of *Giardia.*

geodesic dome: dome-shaped tent with a strong faceted framework of tubular aluminum. Geodesic domes are the Cadillac of domes!

hip belt: a padded waist belt that secures to a backpack — makes carrying the pack much more comfortable.

hollow-ground (knife): the edge is ground to a concave bevel which produces a thin, razor edge and a stiff spine.

hood closure: the tie cord and fastener which secures the hood of a sleeping bag around the sleeper's face.

hypothermia: A potentially lethal physical state caused by lowering of the body's core temperature, due to exposure to cold wet weather. Also called "exposure sickness." See text description.

internal frame pack: a hiking pack with internal stays. The stays give the pack shape and make it more comfortable to carry than a traditional soft pack.

I-pole tent: a tent with a single vertical pole at each end.

Jello-mold oven: an oven made from a large ring aluminum Jello mold. See text description.

kindling: pencil-thin pieces of wood used to nurture a fire to a reliable blaze.

layering: wearing several thin layers of clothes, one over the other. Layering is the most efficient clothing system for cold weather.

lensatic compass: a compass which features a built-in magnifying lens for ease of reading directions. The old army lensatic compass (no longer used) is the best example of this type of instrument. Lensatic compasses are impractical for camping (they don't have built-in protractors), slow to use, and no more accurate than modern Orienteering instruments.

lock-back knife: a folding knife that has an integral lock which "locks" the blade in place when it is open. Some modern lock-backs are really "side-locks" or "front-locks." Lock-back knives do not have pressure springs like ordinary jack-knives, so they can be opened easily with one hand while wearing mittens.

loft: thickness of a sleeping bag that's laying flat and fluffed. Generally speaking, the higher the loft, the warmer the bag.

map index: a specially gridded small-scale map which lists "maps in print," how and where to get them, and their cost. A map index is available free from the U.S. Geological Survey and the Canada Map Office. See text description.

millar-mitts: fingerless gloves used by mountaineers for technical climbing. Millar-mitts are great for fishing, canoeing and general hiking.

mocoa: a popular camp drink which consists of hot-chocolate mixed with coffee.

Moleskin: brand name of soft-surfaced bandaging material used to protect blisters. The sticky side of Moleskin is placed over the unbroken blister; the cushioned surface absorbs the friction from socks and boot.

mountain parka: a generic name for full zipper thigh-length parkas. Mountain parkas usually have lots of pockets. They're traditionally constructed from 60/40 (60 percent nylon, 40 percent cotton) cloth, which is doubled for added warmth. The U.S. Army field jacket is a true mountain parka.

Orienteering: an international sport which combines the skills of map and compass reading with cross-county running.

Orienteering compass: a compass that has a built-in protractor which allows you to determine directions from a map without orienting the map to north. This is the most practical compass style for outdoor use.

overlapping V-tube construction (sleeping bags): a type of baffle construction in which down is secured into V-shaped tubes which overlap one another. Some very warm winter sleeping bags are built this way.

pack basket: a basket pack that's traditionally woven from splints of black ash. This original Indian made item is still going strong in the New England area and is available from L. L. Bean. Pack-baskets are ideal for berry picking, picnicking, canoe trips, and auto camping. They will protect all your breakables. Compared to fabric packs, they are quite inexpensive.

parka: a thigh-length shell garment with integral hood. Parkas may be lined or filled with down, polyester or other insulation for use in cold weather.

pile: a luxuriously soft fabric made from polyester. Pile absorbs little water and it dries quickly if it gets wet. Pile has almost replaced wool as *the* material for cold weather camping.

Polarguard: a synthetic polyester material widely used in sleeping bags and parkas. Polarguard is considered one of the best synthetic insulators.

poly-bottle: short for polyethylene bottle.

poncho: a rectangular, hooded rain garment. Ponchos provide good ventilation and can be worn over a hiking pack. They do not supply reliable protection from rain.

prime: as in "priming" a gasoline or kerosine stove. Stoves are usually primed by filling an integral "spirit cup" with gasoline or alcohol, then setting the fuel aflame.

   Over-prime: Stoves can be "over-primed." If too much gasoline is forced into the spirit-cup, the unit may ignite into a ball of uncontrollable flame.

prismatic compass: a compass with a built-in sighting prism. Prismatic compasses are a step up from lensatic types. They're expensive but not very versatile.

Quallofil: a synthetic material developed by Dupont for use in sleeping bags and parkas. Each filament has four longitudinal holes which trap air and add warmth. *Quallofil* is one of the best synthetic insulators.

quilt construction: a type of sleeping bag construction in which the insulation is sewn (quilt-like) in place. This is an inexpensive way to make a summer weight sleeping bag. This construction is suitable for winter use if the bag is double-quilted.

quick-release knot: a knot which can be removed by a simple pull of the tail. The most common quick-release knot is the "bow" used for tying your shoes.

reflector oven: an aluminum sheet-metal oven which bakes by means of reflected heat. Reflector ovens are hard to keep clean and they are very cumbersome. They require open flame for baking and cannot be used on stoves or over charcoal. They are very efficient if you have a nice bright fire.

ridge-vent: the triangular window at the ridge of A-frame tents.

rip-stop nylon: a lightweight nylon fabric that has heavier threads sewn in at approximate one-quarter-inch intervals. Rip-stop is less likely to tear than taffeta but it has less resistance to abrasion.

seam-sealer: a special glue, available at all camping shops, used to waterproof the stitching on tents and raingear.

Sixty-forty parka: a parka made from fabric which consists of 60 percent nylon and 40 percent cotton. The term "60/40" is now generic; it defines any mountain style parka, regardless of the fabric composition. See "mountain parka."

shell (garments): refers to unlined garments, or the interior or exterior wall of a sleeping bag.

self-supporting tent: theoretically, a tent which needs no staking. However, all self-supporting tents must be staked or they'll blow away in wind.

semi-mummy bag: a sleeping bag with a barrel-shape and no hood. A good choice for those who feel confined by the mummy shape but want lighter weight and more warmth than that supplied by standard rectangular sleeping bags.

sewn-through construction: same as "quilt" construction.

side-wall baffle: a baffle that is opposite the zipper on a sleeping bag; it keeps the down from shifting along the length of the bag.

siwash: a turn-of-the-century term that means to live off the land with a bare minimum of essentials. Modern campers do not siwash!

snow-flaps: ear-like flaps which are sewn to the perimeter of a tent floor. Snow-flaps are folded outward then piled with snow. This eliminates the need for staking the tent. Snow-flaps are an extra-cost feature of special purpose winter tents.

sou'wester: the traditional rain hat of sailors and commercial fishermen. The sou'wester was developed centuries ago and it is still the best of all foul weather hats. The best sou'westers have ear flaps, chin strap, and a flannel lining.

space filler-cut: where the inner and outer shells of a sleeping bag are cut the same size. This construction allows the inner liner and fill to better conform to the curves of your body than the Thermos bottle shape of the "differential cut." The merits/demerits of space-filler versus differential cut are still being argued by sleeping bag manufacturers.

space-blanket: a mylar-coated "blanket" used in survival kits. Space-blankets are waterproof and are very warm for their size and weight. Every camping shop has them.

spreader-bar: same as a "wand." Used for spreading out a portion of a tent.

sternum strap: a short nylon strap which connects the shoulder straps of a hiking pack. A properly adjusted sternum strap transfers some of the pack load to the chest.

storm-flap: a panel of material which backs the zipper of a parka — prevents "the storm" from getting in.

stuff sack: traditionally, a nylon sack in which a sleeping bag is stored. The term now defines any nylon bag with drawstring closure.

Swiss Army knife: originally, the issue knife of the Swiss Army. Now, generic for any "Scout-style" multi-tool pocket knife.

Svea: brand name of the venerable *Svea* stove.

tinder: ultra-fine dry material used for starting a fire.

topo map: a "topographic" map which shows the lay of the land by means of contour lines.

toque: a jaunty wool stocking cap traditionally worn by the Voyageurs.

trenching (also called "ditching"): digging a trench around a tent to carry away ground water which accumulates during a heavy rain. This form of guttering is illegal in all wilderness areas. Ground cloths and tent floors have eliminated the need to "trench" tents. See STORMPROOFING YOUR TENT in the text, for details.

tumpline: a headstrap used to carry heavy loads. Voyageurs carried hundreds of pounds of furs with only a tumpline. Today this feature is found only on traditional canvas duluth packs which are used for wilderness canoeing.

twist-on-a-stick: baking powder bread made by twisting dough on a stick and baking it over the fire.

vestibule: an alcove or extension which secures to one or both ends of a tent. Vestibules provide a place to store gear out of the weather.

Wachita stone: a medium-hard mineral oil stone used for sharpening knives.

wind-shirt: differs from a wind-parka in that the shirt is cut to waist length and does not have a hood. *Wind pants* are made of breathable fabric and are popular for winter camping.

white-print map: a provisional map that's similar to a "blue-print." White-prints are up-to-date maps which show the location of logging and mining roads and man made structures. These maps are designed for professional use; they are not listed in standard map indexes. See text description.

Appendix B

Mail Order Supply Houses

There are many good mail order supply houses. The ones listed below are those with which I've personally done business. They offer top-shelf merchandise, good service, and a fair guarantee.

L.L. Bean, Inc.
Freeport, Maine 04033

A delightful company that does business in the old world tradition. The "Maine Hunting Shoe" (Bean boot) remains one of the most practical and versatile boots for camping. Free catalog.

Indiana Camp Supply, Inc.
P.O. Box 211
Hobart, Indiana 46342,

Your best source of medical items. *Indiana Camp* has the most practical first-aid kits on the market. Their free catalog also lists a wealth of hard-to-find practical gear. *Very fast* service!

Northwest River Supplies
P.O. Box 9186
Moscow, Idaho 83843-9186

Mostly products for river rafters, but also a wealth of water-proof bags and practical products for self-propelled campers.

Recreational Equipment, Inc.
P.O. Box C-88125
Seattle, WA 98188

REI is a co-op. You pay a couple bucks to join then enjoy a yearly dividend on your purchases. REI has a very complete product line, and prices tend to be lower than the competition (especially with membership rebate).

CAMPMOR
810 Route 17 North
P.O. Box 999
Paramus, New Jersey 07653-0999

Very complete product line and reasonable prices. Good source of yard goods, tents and packs. Many hard-to-find items.

PATAGONIA, Inc.
P.O. Box 86
Ventura, CA 93002

PATAGONIA has some of the most beautiful, luxurious, and practical clothing around. Their raingear is unbeatable, as is their pile. Yvon Chouinard, president and founder of PATAGONIA, is a world class mountaineer turned kayaker. The company's designs reflect Chouinard's in-depth knowledge of backcountry conditions. PATAGONIA products are expensive but worth it.

E & B Marine
980 Gladys Ct.
P.O. Box 747
Edison, NJ 08818

This is strictly a boating catalog, however, it contains some very useful camping gear. E & B Marine rain gear is wonderful stuff (suitable for ocean sailing) and is very inexpensive.

CANNONDALE, Inc.
9 Brookside Place
Georgetown, CT 06829

CANNONDALE manufactures world-class bicycle equipment. Their "Aroostook" tent is among the best in the world — most weatherproof tent I've used.

Forestry Suppliers, Inc.
205 West Rankin St.
P.O. Box 8397
Jackson, Mississippi 39204

A 568 page "wish book" that contains virtually everything used by forestry professionals. You'll find everything from axes to wood stoves. This is your most complete source of compasses, map aids and technical equipment.

Johnson Camping, Inc.
One Marine Midland Plaza
P.O. Box 966
Binghamton, NY 13902

This gigantic equipment complex offers Eureka tents, Silva compasses, and Old Town Canoes.

Precise, Inc.
3 Chestnut St.
Suffern, NY 10901

Distributors of high quality imported knives, Suunto compasses, and the reasonably priced "Phoenix" trail stoves.

Sierra West
6 East Yanonali St.
Santa Barbara, CA 93101

A variety of outdoor gear including EVA (ethyl-vinyl-acetate) foam trail pads. Sierra West makes the most comfortable open-cell trail pad around.

Fast Bucksaw Co.
110 East 5th St.
Hastings, MN 55033

Manufacturer of the absolute best folding trail saw (a work of art!).

CABELA'S, Inc.
P.O. Box 199
812 Thirteenth Ave.
Sidney, Nebraska 69162

A diversity of camping products, keyed mostly to the hunter and fisherman.

THE SKI HUT
P.O. Box 309
1615 University Ave.
Berkeley, CA 94701

The Ski Hut manufactures Trailwise equipment, extolled by
Colin Fletcher in his book *The Complete Walker*. Trailwise gear
is impeccably fashioned, honestly useful, and very expensive. Free
catalog.

INDEX

153